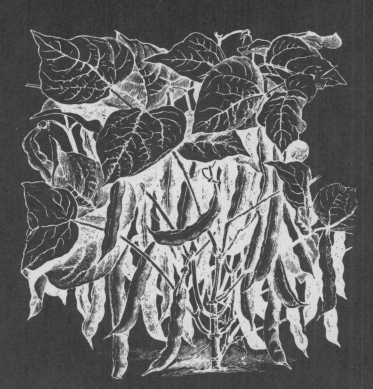

TO DWELL IS TO GARDEN

TO DWELL IS TO GARDEN

A History of Boston's Community Gardens

SAM BASS WARNER, JR.

Photographs by Hansi Durlach

Northeastern University Press

BOSTON

Northeastern University Press

Library of Congress Cataloging in Publication Data

Warner, Sam Bass, 1928–
To dwell is to garden.

Includes index.
1. Community gardens—Massachusetts—Boston—
History. 2. Community gardens—History. 3. Community
gardens—Massachusetts—Boston—Pictorial works.
4. Gardeners—Massachusetts—Boston—Pictorial works.
5. Vegetable gardening—Massachusetts—Boston.
I. Durlach, Hansi. II. Title.
SB457.3.W37 1987   630′.9744′61   86–23898
ISBN 1-55553-007-9 (alk. paper)

Designed by David Ford.

Composed in Century Expanded by Graphic Composition,
Athens, Georgia.

The photographic insert was printed duotone by Meriden Gravure,
Meriden, Connecticut, on Warren's Lustro Dull, an acid-free sheet.

The text was printed and bound by Halliday Lithograph,
Hanover, Massachusetts. The text paper is Warren's Olde Style,
an acid-free sheet.

Manufactured in the United States of America
91 90 89 88 87   5 4 3 2 1

to Charlotte Kahn and George Goethals

CONTENTS

v i i

viii

ACKNOWLEDGMENTS

Community gardening is not a subject embraced by a single department of scholars. Its activities range across the specialties of city planning, landscape architecture, horticulture, botany, nutrition, urban history, and evolution. Indeed, one of the aims of this book is to assemble bibliographic information on the very diverse literatures that touch upon community gardening.

To accomplish this task we have drawn upon the time and experience of many scholars and friends. We should especially like to thank David Smith of Washington, D.C., Dovi Birnbaum of Newton, Massachusetts, Anne Whiston Spirn and Setha Low of the University of Pennsylvania, Roger Montgomery of the University of California at Berkeley, Jonathan Spence of Yale, Pier Paula Penzo of the University of Bologna, Italy, Charles A. Lewis of the Morton Arboretum in Lisle, Illinois, William E. Warner of the *North Carolina Independent*, and Boston University colleagues Gillian Cooper-Driver, George K. Lewis, Roy A. Glasgow, Joseph Boskin, and Thomas F. Glick.

We should also like to thank the staffs of the libraries who were so generous in their help: the Harvard Graduate School of Design, Rotch Library of the Massachusetts Institute of Technology, the Massachusetts Horticultural Society, and especially Emily Clark of the Newberry Library, Chicago, and Alice Bowen of the M.I.T. Library.

The photographic portfolio has required the assistance of many persons. The publication of the photographs has been made possible by a generous grant from Cabot, Cabot & Forbes of Boston. And special thanks must go to Nancy Borden, for permission to use some of her oral history material, and to Charlotte Kahn, Marc Mills, Ken Ryan, Beth Arndtsen, and Edward Cooper of Boston Urban Gardeners, and above all to the many Boston community gardeners who gave so generously of their time and without whose enthusiasm and cooperation this project would not have been possible.

Hansi Durlach
Sam Bass Warner, Jr.

ix

PREFACE

This is an unusual book because, as it examines the community gardens of one city, it draws upon all of human history and reports on worldwide events. It was surprising to us, a historian and a photographer, that everyday activities taking place on the vacant lots of Boston should strike such resonances, but they do. The clearing of rubble and trash, the planting of seeds, the weeding and watering and harvesting of vegetables for family kitchens are all central human tasks that mean much more than you might first imagine. But the depth of human meaning is there and, if you will consider these tasks in the framework of people seeking food and land and building cities, the many meanings will come to you and the resonances of space and time will grow stronger and stronger.

The multiple meanings of essential tasks are what we discovered in the vacant lot gardens of Boston. We offer this book so that others can share in our discoveries. The process began for us four years ago when, as a director of Boston Urban Gardeners, I told my friend Hansi Durlach that interesting and important things were happening on the abandoned lots of the city. Months later she returned full of excitement at the first discovery: the community gardeners of Boston were a fascinating mix of people from all over the world—from China, from Chile, from Italy, from Canada, from Arkansas, from the suburbs, and from next door.

Hansi's beautiful portraits reminded us both of the rural photographs taken during the 1930s by the crews of the Farm Service Administration. There is an important difference, however. Hers are not documentary pictures taken for a Washington file or a New York magazine. Every picture published here is a reproduction of a 16 × 20-inch photograph Durlach has given to the gardeners themselves. In addition, here the subjects speak. In Part Two of this book we offer both a selection of Durlach's community garden portraits and excerpts from her conversations with her subjects. These portraits and statements are the essential links between the city's streetside gardens and the world.

The second discovery occurred when I was watching a slide presentation at the Suffolk

County Agricultural Service offices. An M.I.T. student had talked with Boston gardeners and had made a nice slide show from his interviews. As I listened to an Afro-American woman tell about the vegetables she was growing, I suddenly realized that she had within her 10 × 15-foot plot a history of her people: the melons and okra from Africa, the green beans and squashes from the American Indians, and the collards brought from England by the slave masters.

I thought that if I only knew the history of the vegetables themselves, their history would tell me of the movement of people across the world and their exchanges with one another, and ultimately I would come to the migrations to America and the arrivals in my city. The report on this discovery forms the last part of the book: "The Histories within the Gardens." There, in Part Three, the common vegetables are arranged into five groups, each one representing a different history and migration experience: the Anglo-Irish garden, the Afro-American garden, the Italian garden, the Chinese garden, and the Hispanic garden.

Further discoveries came directly out of historical research. They were the discovery of the politics of city building and the politics of garden land. It is perfectly clear to any city dweller that the land for community gardens, the new open spaces and vacant lots, is the product of suburbanization. The emptying out of the formerly dense cities, the diffusion of the contemporary metropolitan America which has been rushing on since World War II, cleared the buildings off patches of inner-city land. Thousands upon thousands of Americans abandoned their cities, and as they did so they left rubble-filled lots on the sites of their former houses. This is the land the community gardeners have transformed from health and safety problems into tools for a humane style of urban living.

The discovery of the history of urban land came from reading descriptions of cities in Europe and towns in the United States during the seventeenth and eighteenth centuries. These old human settlements were full of gardened land. Most commonly the gardens were behind rows of houses, open narrow backyards, and there were also fields of gardens set against the inside edge of the city walls. But, as in today's inner-city neighborhood, there were patches of open space scattered everywhere. The third discovery was the realization of the meaning of these old places. Here was an older way of building a city. The city of bricks and asphalt which many of us remember from our youth was not the inevitable way to build cities, but instead a bad mutation brought on by nineteenth- and twentieth-century land greed. Throughout most of history human beings have built their cities with gardens and open spaces. Indeed a philosopher taught me that our old word "to dwell" fused two older words that had two distinct meanings: to build and to cultivate the land.[1]

The fourth discovery also came from reading about the eighteenth century. I was seeking the origins of community gardens by asking a question about a pattern of land use:

where else, and at what earlier times, did landless people cultivate small garden plots in grouped parcels separated from their homes? The answer turned up in a nasty bit of English history. At about the time of the American Revolution the farmers and landlords of England divided and fenced the common lands of the villages, thereby driving thousands of country families into poverty and on to public relief. Community gardens, vegetable plots offered at very low rents, then commenced as a philanthropic experiment undertaken in the hope of reducing the costs of public welfare! The present-day, well-established national and municipal community garden programs of northern European countries have their origins in this unpleasant bit of charity.

And so came the realization that, although community gardening may be two hundred years old, the politics of American community gardeners is new. The recent American community garden movement is propelled by groups of neighbors who organize themselves to clear or secure their own land and to maintain their garden parcels. It is a politics of self-help and local empowerment, not a politics of charity or reform of the poor. Its immediate origin, in fact, turned out to be the civil rights movement of the 1960s. The report of these two discoveries, the politics of city building and the politics of community garden land, is given as the opening themes of the book: without politics or land there are no gardens.

NOTE TO THE PREFACE

1. Martin Heidegger, *Poetry, Language, Thought*, ed. Albert Hofstadter (New York, 1971), 146.

We've left something of ourselves here.
When you've planted a garden, you've left
something permanent.
They can't take that away from you—
no matter what,
short of digging up the land.
But other than that
the land which remains here,
even if nobody tended this garden for years,
something would remain here,
something would still be growing here
that we had something to do with.
And you could come back here
and look at it and smile.

EVELYN MCMAHON

PART ONE
A History of
Community Gardening

IN CHARLESTOWN, MASSACHUSETTS,

on the far side of the famous Revolutionary battleground, on the back slope next to the site of the former elevated railway terminal, the city streets converge into an industrial crossroads. Here still stands the giant Schrafft's candy factory, now awaiting new tenants, and although weeds have grown up on the traffic rotary and have overrun many vacant properties nearby, this intersection, Sullivan Square, remains an industrial thoroughfare for the trucks and business of Boston harbor. In one of the triangles formed by the convergence of Medford and Bunker Hill streets, the Boston Redevelopment Authority seized a large parcel of land, about two acres, and tore down the nest of old houses that formerly had crowded the site. For years thereafter the property stood vacant, gathering trash, weeds, and rats. No private purchaser for the cleared land appeared to renew the property. House restoration and construction in Charlestown was taking place on the other side of the hill, where attractive old houses and a historic aura still lingered.

In the spring of 1976 a newcomer to Charlestown, Nina Gomez Ibanez began to garden on this vacant lot. Ms. Ibanez was a woman of suburban gardening experience who had no land next to her apartment on Concord Street. She enlisted as her gardening partner James Hall, a Polaroid employee, who had a backyard garden at his home on Green Street and who was an avid cultivator. Together during the spring and summer of 1976 Ms. Ibanez and Mr. Hall cleared off one former houselot and set out ten plots to begin a community vegetable garden. Year by year the Sullivan Square gardeners buried more and more of the builders' rubble that had been dumped on the site, and cleared and planted more land. In 1978 the group took the name Gardeners for Charlestown, and they began to expand their functions by supplying local residents with soil for window-boxes and vegetable seedlings.

Today there are seventy 10 × 10-foot plots and sixty-five gardeners cultivating the one-third-acre corner of the unused parcel. Ms. Ibanez has returned to the suburbs and Mr. Hall has succeeded to the leadership of the project, where he has carried out an ambitious planting program, setting out lawn borders, planting fruit trees and vines, and even starting a small nursery. His fellow gardeners reflect the recent history of this section of Boston: some are old residents of Irish descent like Mr. Hall, others are newcomers from the suburbs, and others are immigrants from Korea and the Philippines.

For twenty-one years these two acres in Sullivan Square have stood vacant, the property of the Boston Redevelopment Authority. Nearby are weedy, abandoned lots and some derelict tenements which cry out for rebuilding or replacement. For ten years one corner of this land has been in active use by local community gardeners. The gardeners, however, have done their work without any security of tenure, without any lease or formal agreement from the municipal owner. Two years ago the BRA decided that the reconstruction of Charlestown had advanced far enough so that a private developer could

3

be sought to purchase the land. The Bricklayers' Union responded with a proposal to destroy the garden and to cover the entire lot with housing. Mr. Hall and his gardeners responded with a signature campaign; the city-wide league of community gardeners, Boston Urban Gardeners, joined in the defense; there was television and newspaper coverage; and after a public hearing in Charlestown the bricklayers' proposal was rejected. The Redevelopment Authority then adjusted its request for proposals, saying that future designs for new housing should include a community garden. At this writing proposals are being submitted, some of which leave the garden at its present site, others of which require that it be begun again in a different corner of the parcel.[1]

This Charlestown case is unusual only to the degree that the garden has been landscaped and long-term plantings instituted. It is not the sort of annual vegetable garden that can be easily relocated. Indeed, the case resembles the garden of Adam Purple in the lower East Side of New York City.[2] There an eccentric gardener built an elaborate garden on an abandoned lot, and the municipal authorities wantonly destroyed it in order to demonstrate their power. As in Charlestown so in New York: nearby lots stood vacant, offering ample space for the construction of new housing. In Charlestown the garden sits at the apex of a triangle of land that is next to the heaviest truck traffic and therefore is the least desirable location for houses. To require the garden to be moved therefore does not serve to improve a housing site plan. But more important than the formal criteria of site design, moving the garden will not meet the most important goal of making Charlestown more habitable. This small corner of land has been for the past decade the site of Charlestown residents' own voluntary urban renewal. To refuse to recognize the worth and the legitimacy of their activities, and to refuse to grant formal security of tenure to the garden association is to use the state and municipal powers of eminent domain to make the city less habitable than it was prior to public intervention twenty-one years ago.

The Charlestown gardeners are a small group among millions of city dwellers around the world. Everywhere landless people are seeking space to grow food for their families and a place to put up a shelter. They find room on the wastes and fringes of cities—in vacant lots, along railroads and highways, in rough land unfit for commercial agriculture, and on the cast-offs at the outer edges of urban expansion.

To control this land, which commonly they do not own or lease, the gardeners band together into informal associations that establish the lot boundaries, streets, and paths, obtain water, and often, as well, govern what becomes a squatter settlement.

In a few nations land for vegetable plots is provided by public authorities through leases to gardeners' associations, but most commonly the gardeners are temporary occupants of unused land who depend upon government toleration or after-the-fact consent.

Often, too, gardening and squatting are part of an ongoing urban warfare in which the police and the army are called in to devastate the gardens and to drive off the gardeners.

Throughout Asia there is intense cultivation of urban land, but apparently no informal associations of gardeners as in Latin America or Europe. In Central and South America, and in Africa—paradoxically, all continents where land abounds—the community gardeners are rural migrants struggling to find places for themselves in settings of explosive urbanization.[3] Northern Europe faced a similar political and social situation one and two centuries ago. There popular programs of self-help merged with the programs of philanthropists to establish government policies for public support of urban gardening.

Today the United States stands in confusion between the two extremes of Latin America and northern Europe. Across the nation landless people have taken up the cultivation of vegetables on the vacant lots of their cities and suburbs. Public response to this self-help has been mixed. As a rich nation which does not respect those of its citizens who are poor, many Americans dismiss these city gardens as insignificant activities: temporary uses to be tolerated only during the interval between land clearance and new construction. Government officials and private landowning citizens deny the legitimacy of vegetable and flower gardens as permanent uses for urban land. On the other hand, most Americans are suburbanites, and most of these citizens have lawns and gardens to tend. The American suburbs, also, are home to many active participants in world ecological campaigns. From these sources come sympathy for urban community gardening and some of the same philanthropic energies that fostered the garden policies of northern Europe.[4]

There are as well two special elements in the current position of the United States. The political force of community gardening does not rest upon philanthropy but springs from a new kind of local politics that grew out of the civil rights movement. This politics emphasizes self-help, and it insists on the dignity of all participants. The civil rights tradition has made it possible for welfare mothers, newcomers from the suburbs, and overseas immigrants to join together in garden associations. The second special element in the current position pertains to the condition of center-city land itself. Community gardening is most often vacant lot gardening. It follows after twenty-five years of abandonment of inner-city properties. Until the very recent revival of inner-city real estate markets the nation enjoyed a double opportunity that did not exist in the European past. First, there was the opportunity to recognize the new gardening politics as part of an American tradition of personal dignity and self-help, and, second, there was a chance to use the gardens themselves as elements in urban reconstruction. Although public authorities across the nation have lately been closing out community gardens, there is still time to recognize and to encourage the gardeners' politics, and there is still plenty of inner-city land for both new gardens and new houses.

Even as we observe these fresh opportunities, we are appalled by the ignorance of the general public and their public authorities concerning both the history of cities and the history of urban gardening. Neither the general public nor the mayors and their staffs know enough of the past to realize that cities without gardens are the products of exceptional circumstances, a sort of bad mutation brought on by the land rush of the 1750–1930 era. The past cities of brick, asphalt, and concrete that they hold up to us all as the models of human prosperity are in fact the junkyards of shortsighted land profiteering, a take-the-money-and-run approach to city building. An example from Boston's experience reveals the false premises that are currently used to attack the open spaces which gardeners cultivate. This case involves a politically invisible garden—a small, informal vegetable garden which is fenced about with scrap wire and old boards. Passersby can scarcely notice it because it stands behind a row of parked cars and next to an abandoned factory amidst the vacant industrial lots of Boston's South End. As in the Charlestown case, this garden uses one vacant lot in an area of many vacant lots. The gardeners are politically as invisible as their garden because they are Puerto Ricans who dwell in the housing project across the street. They are not the sort of people television crews and newspaper reporters find easily.

The current history of the garden began in 1949 with a housing project. Two blocks of old brick tenements which had been the unwelcoming reception houses for Boston's turn-of-the-century immigrants were cleared away. The project, located between Washington Street and Harrison Avenue, stands next to the Cathedral of the Holy Cross (built between 1867 and 1875), from which it gets its name, Cathedral South End Housing Project. Although it was intended as an aid to the poor of the city and was one of several projects constructed to relieve the post–World War II housing shortage, federal specifications required that it be built at a level below the commonplace standards of its day. It is, accordingly, short of usable open space, and it offers its 508 families no place for sports, car repair, or gardening, all everyday activities of Boston residents.[5]

In 1965 the Boston Redevelopment Authority began tearing down old buildings in the South End to clear off sites for the private construction of new housing. In the process it leveled the ends of several city blocks adjacent to the Cathedral project. Then, as in Charlestown, satisfactory private developers did not come forward, so that these lots commenced a decade of accumulation of builders' rubble, trash, weeds, and rats. The unused land also attracted speculators who began purchasing such properties at low prices to hold for later development or resale. Since such speculations deprived the Redevelopment Authority of full control over future development, the authority instituted a policy of developer designation to forestall the speculators. By this practice a particular firm was designated as the developer, the BRA set a price for the land, and it began to enter into planning agreements with the named party.

Meanwhile the land stood vacant, a nuisance and a hazard to those who lived nearby.

A decade later, a decade after the land had been seized by the City, in the spring and summer of 1976, civil rights, antiwar, and environmental activists formed a coalition in Boston for the construction of community gardens in the South End. The small garden at the end of the Harrison Avenue, Plympton, East Dedham, and Albany streets block was one of these initial community gardens. The Massachusetts National Guard trucked in topsoil as a volunteer activity, and Don Rico, a blind resident of the Cathedral project, took charge as the first garden leader. The coalition arranged for a water spigot, the gardeners found scraps for a fence, and gardening began that summer. Since then the twenty-odd plots of the garden have served the Cathedral project residents as an important source of food and as a place to exercise their competence as gardeners.

A vegetable garden of annuals, a place of beans, peppers, tomatoes, eggplant, cilantro, and potatoes can easily be relocated. Many lots stand vacant near the Cathedral project, several of which could serve as open spaces and gardens for the project residents. Yet the way the public authorities have been managing the vacant land next to the project for the past twenty years suggests that they do not hold the values of making the city habitable high in their minds. Despite the underdesign of the project, no formal action has been taken to develop vacant parcels for residents' use. Instead, an industrial corporation was named as the designated developer. First, New England Nuclear was designated and that company proposed to construct an office building on the garden site. Then E. I. Du Pont of Wilmington, Delaware, purchased New England Nuclear and paved over its own open land to make large parking lots. At this writing the Boston Redevelopment Authority has written the new corporation to ask what its intentions for the development of the garden site might be. Surely the needs of inner-city residents for garden space and open space next to their homes should take precedence over parking. Yet in a political contest a giant industrial corporation seemingly has the advantage over a group of Puerto Rican migrants and public housing residents, no matter how legitimate their case.[6]

Such examples as these, the elaborate garden of Charlestown and the modest one of the South End, are now repeated across the nation. During the past decade community gardeners in American cities cleared acres of vacant trash-filled land and returned it to useful activity. Most of these gardens now lack the protection of ownership, long-term leases, or an established favorable municipal policy. Most are threatened by the same city-destructive policies that threaten the community gardens of Boston.[7]

The Origins of Community Gardens in England

Modern community gardening first appeared in England, during the eighteenth century, because that country was the world's first modern nation. There the countryside was transformed into a totally fenced land of commercial farms. Simultaneously the cities of

England were constructed as blocks upon blocks of built-up streets of narrow workers' houses, unrelieved by open spaces or gardens. Both the rural and the urban changes denied thousands of people access to land that they had formerly depended upon for food and pleasure. This denial, in turn, brought forward two modern social responses: philanthropy and self-help. In the countryside wealthy landowners began to offer small parcels for lease to farm laborers as community gardens; and in the cities artisans banded together to rent fringe land so that they could raise vegetables and flowers. After a century the two movements merged into a national policy for the municipal provision of land for community gardening.

The philanthropic side of community gardening was a response to the devastating results of a new rural practice—the private enclosure of what had formerly been common land. In the eighteenth century rural England was covered with farm villages, each one of which combined several sorts of land. There were fenced forests and farms that belonged to private owners, there were open fields to which a number of families had cultivation rights, and there were village commons and village pastures, waste lands, fields, marshes, and forests that all village residents were entitled to use.

According to long-standing customs, village residents—landless laborers as well as small tenants—had the right to keep a cow or pig and to cut wood for fuel or timbers for housebuilding in the nearby commons and waste lands. Often as well they tended small patches of potatoes and vegetables in the open village fields. The patchwork of cultivated and waste lands of the typical English village included both the undocumented customary practices of the lesser families and the documented titles of the large farmers and landlords.

Then, in the face of new techniques for systematic commercial agriculture, the large farmers began to petition Parliament for enclosure acts, which authorized the division of open fields, waste lands, and commons into separate private parcels. To receive a share in these divisions a person had to prove some established title. The laborers and the small tenants who used the commons and the waste lands by custom, without written leases or titles, received nothing. Many others were granted such small bits and pieces that they gladly sold their fragments to the large farmers for a little cash.

Thus rural land in England was fenced during the decades when the United States first began as a separate nation. In the span of years from the French and Indian Wars of 1754 to the termination of the Napoleonic Wars in 1815, England went through its first great convulsions of agricultural transformation, urbanization, and industrialization. Eight thousand square miles of land were enclosed by special parliamentary acts—an area equivalent to one-seventh of all of England, an area the size of all the land in Massachusetts![8] Young people flocked to the new industrial towns and to London, while many of those who could afford passage to America emigrated to seek a fresh start here. But thousands of formerly self-sufficient families remained stranded in the villages of England, reduced to seasonal farm labor and local poor relief. The welfare statistics of the day told of the massive destruction of human resources: in 1750 the local relief bill for all of England totaled £700,000, but by 1818 it had soared to £8,000,000.[9]

The impoverishment of so many rural families set off a ceaseless, grinding, and progressively demeaning debate, the very sort of debate we still carry on today. Having turned rural society upside down and uprooted thousands of families, the very country landowners who initiated the rural revolution complained of the rising costs of welfare and its burden upon local property taxes. Fearful for the future, England experienced a wave of nostalgia, and both radical and conservative politicians joined in lamenting the loss of the good old days of village England prior to the enclosures. That was a time, they imagined, when everyone had a place, and lord, farmer, tenant, and laborer each knew his duties and his privileges.[10]

Charitable organizations sprang up to propose public remedies. William Wilberforce, England's leader in the campaign to abolish slavery in the empire's colonies, established a Society for Bettering the Condition and Increasing the Comforts of the Poor in 1796. His society proposed that landless villagers be given small parcels of land to cultivate.[11] Twenty years later a similar organization, the Laborers' Friend Society, was founded to continue this campaign for the creation of village allotments of a size sufficient to allow a man to feed an entire family on the produce.[12]

Farmers, the men who hired the rural poor, stood in opposition to such proposals for making even little plots available to the landless. They feared that their laborers would spend too much time gardening on their own account, or that they would become independent enough to force up their wages. In this opposition to village gardens the farmers were joined by contemporary economic publicists. For example, the public health reformer Edwin Chadwick opposed gardens because he thought they would encourage the poor to remain in their home villages instead of moving about in search of employment.[13]

The famous political economist John Stuart Mill opposed allotment gardens because he saw them as rewarding the least ambitious young country families. He thought the little village gardens would cause the shiftless to rest in their villages, to garden, and to have babies, and thereby so to multiply that in time they would impoverish all of England by their incontinence and their improvidence.[14]

Mill's was an early expression of the same anger we hear expressed toward the poor and the unfortunate results of their poverty and ignorance. He could not see the poor people of rural England as part of the harvest of the new commercial agriculture, any more than most of us can now see poor, young welfare mothers as part of the output of our metropolitan offices and factories. Yet so they were in Mill's time; and so they are in ours. Shoved to the edges of villages, and to the alleys and courts of cities, neglected, their labor devalued, ill-trained and unrewarded, they made human lives as best they could from the leftovers of a hard-driving society that was running away from them.[15]

At first, during the late eighteenth century, a few very wealthy peers, men with vast estates who had observed the consequences of their own enclosures, began to set aside patches of small gardens which they rented cheaply to their villagers. These were the first allotment gardens, gardens separate from people's cottages, gardens "allotted" to villagers. These were the rural ancestors of today's urban community gardens.[16] Such examples, set as they were by aristocratic landowners, encouraged local charity boards to rent and divide small fields to sublet to poor families as a supplement to the village cash relief. It proved a practical, if ungenerous, charity, and in 1819 Parliament passed an act that encouraged the poor wardens of England to lease up to twenty acres of land for the purpose of subletting as garden plots, or "potato gardens," as they were sometimes called.[17]

Village gardens were never freely offered. Instead, the charitable allotments always included expressions of public anger at the poor. And they were restricted by special rules. A typical example of commonplace regulations were those governing these allotments of one-eighth acre:

> No occupier will be allowed to plow his land, but be required to cultivate it solely by spade husbandry.
>
> No occupier who is at work for the parish, or for any employer, will be allowed to work upon his land after six o'clock in the morning, or before six o'clock in the evening without permission from his master.
>
> All occupiers will be expected to attend regularly at Divine service, to conduct themselves with propriety at all times; and to bring up their families in a decent and orderly manner.[18]

And, of course, the rent had to be paid yearly. Yet so widespread was the desire of the poor of England for land that thousands took up gardens and small plots under such demeaning terms. No matter how many left for the mill towns and cities of England, or emigrated to the United States, there were not jobs enough to maintain the country people remaining. Rioting by angry farm laborers during the 1830s, and then devastating failures of the potato crop in Ireland and on the Continent, brought starvation and suffering to millions. As a consequence, in England rural allotments became a regular feature of village charity. Indeed, in 1845 Parliament required that thereafter fields of allotment gardens be established as a precondition attending all subsequent enclosures.[19] A survey in 1873 counted 244,000 allotments, a third of these the large size advocated by the Laborers' Friend Society, plots of one-quarter to four acres in size.[20]

After a century of enclosures, a century of refashioning commercial farms, a century of growth of mill towns and industrial cities, and a century of charity politics, the rural population of England ceased to be either a significant fraction of the nation's population or a significant political force. The attention of business, politics, and charity now shifted to the city. Here allotment gardens faced different circumstances and even for a time flourished outside the politics of charity.

Urban Self-Help

During the same decades of rural enclosures, the cities of England boomed with the stimulation of new industrial practices and new factory production. This urban expansion called forth the second element in community gardening's history—the tradition of self-help. In England, as throughout the world and throughout history, town dwellers had always been gardeners. Kitchen gardens, fruit trees, and vines, were necessary elements in town and city life.[21] Until the tidal waves of population flows and the great urban real estate booms of the late eighteenth and early nineteenth centuries, most city blocks held patches of open spaces, backyards of sorts, which residents cultivated as kitchen gardens. These open spaces were the common places of traditional modes of bit-by-bit city building. In 1794 Thomas Pemberton described Boston as being just such a place: "Few houses are without them [garden spots] in which vegetables and flowers are raised, [and] in some fruit trees planted."[22]

At the time no one appreciated the important contributions these open spaces made to the ecologies of towns.[23] We now know that these rear yards helped to absorb a good deal of the human and animal wastes of the city, that they provided significant amounts of food, milk, and eggs, and that they helped to offset the bad drainage and coal-fouled air that prevailed in these centuries. Then during the late eighteenth century the yards and open spaces disappeared when landlords filled them with dark courts and alleys, and when developers ran up row after row of small attached houses, each one with a tiny rear yard scarcely large enough to afford a privy and a coal bin.[24] These new building practices made the city into a death trap for poor people, and it took a century of public reform—massive and costly water, sewer, and street engineering—to overcome these public consequences of private ignorance and greed.[25]

Confronted by the new city landlessness, city dwellers clubbed together to rent plots on the edge of town where they tended family gardens. The manufacturing city of Birmingham was famous for its neat and carefully laid out "guinea gardens," gardens so named for the price of their annual rent.[26] A newspaper in 1812 carried an advertisement for the sale of one of these gardens, "well planted with gooseberry and currant trees, fine raspberries, flowers, shrubs, etc., and stocked with asparagus and vegetables of various kinds [and] containing a summer house."[27] Nottingham, another mill city, had a development parallel to Birmingham's. That town now claims that its hosiery workers held England's first rose show at an inn next to their gardens.[28] The shortcomings in these arrangements lay in their vulnerability. As cities grew, the landlords sold off the gardens for railway yards, roads, and housing developments. Thus, in time the gardeners had to seek land ever farther from the center of town, and land for gardening often became impossible to find.[29]

The public benefits that flowed from the commonplace activities of ordinary city dwellers were not discovered. The late eighteenth- and early nineteenth-century workingmen's gardens added a much needed variety to the public spaces and domestic life of town dwellers, but no public action that recognized these general benefits was forthcoming. The garden associations had to contend as best they could with increasing land shortages and rising rents. Rather than coming to their fellow citizens' aid, municipal authorities directed their activities to landscaping for passive appreciation: the beautification of city squares, the erecting of monuments, and the laying out of parks for promenading.

Only the old nasty motives of saving tax money on poor relief and disciplining the working poor convinced municipal governments to undertake allotment programs. During the late nineteenth century several English cities, following earlier village precedents, experimented with welfare allotment gardens. Finally, in 1907 Parliament passed a law calling upon the local governments of England to set up allotment gardens for the "laboring population" where such land could not be obtained by private agreement.[30] This 1907 statute served as the foundation for Britain's now extensive allotment system.

The example of allotment gardens spread from England across northern Europe so that by 1900 all the nations from Switzerland to Norway had garden programs. In Germany the campaign was led by a physician, Daniel G. M. Schreber (1808–61), who wanted fresh air and exercise to promote the health of city children. He formed an alliance with industrialists who were seeking ways to reduce the Sunday drinking of their employees. Factory owners often contributed land for gardens, and they thereby solved a persistent problem of community gardening—finding space for gardens near where the gardeners worked or lived. The Germans laid out generous allotments, 15 × 30 meters (49.2 × 98.4 feet). Here many gardeners eventually built small summer houses for family outings and vacation days. Today these gardens are in keen demand and are known in Germany as "leisure gardens."[31]

In France the promise of garden land for urban workers was also part of a campaign for the reform of the manners and morals of the common people. During the late nineteenth century conservative politicians in France deplored as moral decay the popular habits of late marriage and small families. They saw early marriage, many children, and home ownership as antidotes to labor unions, strikes, and socialist politics. A Christian Democratic movement arose to promote these moral sentiments. Two of its major promises were land for a home and land for a garden for every worker. The houselots were never seriously advanced, but the movement's garden federation, Ligue Française du Coin de Terre et Foyer, did succeed in becoming the recipient of government subsidies for allotment gardens.[32]

In Belgium allotment gardening was also tied to home ownership goals, but in that nation its ties were to workingmen's cooperative banks. In Sweden and Norway large allotment gardens with summer houses became the precedents for municipal schemes for the provision of suburban houselots for city workers. Italy, however, never adopted a national or a municipal allotment garden policy. As in the United States, large manufacturers sometimes built housing with garden space for their workers, but Italy still struggles today to define a policy for urban community gardens in the face of a movement that has sprung up without official sanction.[33]

Beginnings in the United States

The United States started its allotment gardening out of the same desires both to feed and to control the poor as those of England and northern Europe. In our case the trigger was the economic depression of 1893–97. The depression had begun with a rush of money out of the United States, a financial crisis that caused 491 bank failures the first year. As the bad years continued, they affected railroad traffic, and by 1894 one-third of the mileage of American railroads had sunk into bankruptcy. In the late nineteenth century railroads were the core industry of the nation, and when they faltered thousands lost their jobs—just as we have seen a faltering automobile industry send waves of unemployment across the nation. So in 1894–97 armies of young native and immigrant laborers were stranded in cities without work.

Detroit, then a manufacturing city with a specialty in building railroad cars, was one of the cities hard hit by unemployment. Its mayor, Hazen S. Pingree, noticed during the spring of 1894 that few jobs were being posted. He called for owners of vacant land at the edge of the city to lend their property so that the unemployed might at least raise sufficient potatoes to carry their families through the next winter. The real estate business also being slack, 600 acres were promptly tendered. The City of Detroit appropriated money to plow and harrow 430 acres, and the mayor hired a retired U.S. Army officer to supervise the project. That spring 945 families took up allotments, gardens of one-quarter to one-half an acre in size. Each family was issued seed potatoes with instructions to plant at least half the land to that crop. In the fall the gardeners harvested 14,000 bushels of potatoes, and an uncounted crop of beans, turnips, and other vegetables.

Detroit's experience with what were then called Pingree's Potato Patches captured national attention, and a number of cities planned to imitate it the following year. Detroit's first report boasted of the same sort of economies that the wardens of late eighteenth-century England took pleasure in announcing. The city had invested $3,000 in land preparation and supervision, $12,000 worth of crops had been raised, so presumably $9,000 in relief expenditures had been saved for the taxpayers.

The next few years a number of cities offered such potato patches: Boston, Brooklyn,

Buffalo, Chicago, Dayton, Denver, Kansas City, Minneapolis, New York, Omaha, Providence, Reading (Pennsylvania), Seattle, Springfield (Massachusetts), and Toledo. Only Detroit and Buffalo mounted large programs that served one and two thousand families per season; in the other cities the undertakings were small and the number of families given gardens few.[34]

In the United States this first allotment garden movement was trapped within a self-defeating outlook. Both city officials and private charity officers who administered these programs accepted the idea that the American city was first and foremost a real estate proposition, a place where the highest and best use of land was not the raising of human beings but the piling up of profits on rents and sales. It was a time of widespread immigration into cities, the tearing down of old houses to replace them with tall tenements, and the removal of old downtown buildings to erect the first skyscrapers. Density, the sheer crowding of people, was the landlord's profit and the driving idea of city building. Contemporaries, of course, noticed the harsh decline in the habitability of their cities and the attacks on the health and well-being of city families. Reformers saw deconcentration as the only sure remedy and advocated rapid transit construction to open up the suburbs to workingmen's families.[35] Given such times and such an outlook, garden officials could offer neither convenient locations for their gardens nor security of tenure. In this important respect the Americans had yet to understand what the Germans had already mastered: putting the gardens where the people were.

In the United States landowners allowed their land to be plowed and cultivated only on the condition that, should the land be subsequently sold or leased for development, the gardens would be immediately forfeited. Moreover, to their surprise, the managers of the potato patches discovered that their applicants, both native and immigrant, were not predominantly farm people, and many did not know how to grow vegetables. From this necessity for teaching, the charitable committees reasoned that small sites could not be gardened because they could not be supervised conveniently, and therefore that big tracts were required. They could not imagine that the gardeners would be able to teach each other, the novice learning from the experienced. As a consequence of such imperfect specifications, urban land for gardens proved hard to find, especially land near the homes of the unemployed.

Boston's experience showed how such an ill-conceived preference for large plots prevented the philanthropists from establishing a successful program. In 1895 one of the city's oldest private charities, the Industrial Aid Society for the Prevention of Pauperism (founded in 1835), undertook to imitate Mayor Pingree's example. The society, whose specialty was running an employment office, set aside a special fund and set up a special subcommittee, the Committee on the Cultivation of Vacant Lots. Through the committee's appeals many small lots were offered, but the committee chose instead the one large plot scheme. It leased a sixty-acre farm, the Morton Farm, at what was then the outer edge of the city of Boston. The farm was located at the corner of Morton and Canterbury streets, between the Forest Hills Cemetery and the brand-new Franklin Park.

The land had not been farmed for at least twenty-five years,[36] so a "practical farmer," George Starratt, was hired to plow, harrow, and spread phosphate on the land, and to supervise the gardeners for the coming season. Next the subcommittee placed advertisements in the newspapers, and arranged with fifteen offices about the city to receive applications. In the end fifty-two men and two women showed up at Morton Farm and were assigned one-third-acre plots. Planting began May 20 and lasted until June 10. Each gardener was required to sow a row of beans at the outer edges of his garden to mark the boundary, and then to put in many rows of potatoes. The other vegetables raised were corn, peas, turnips, cabbage, cucumbers, tomatoes, and melons.[37]

Most of the gardeners turned out to be "men physically unable to do a full day's work, which fact prevented them from taking permanent employment." Comments in this first 1895 report and those of the following years suggest that most of these gardeners were old men. As in other cities, most of the gardeners were native born, and the national origins of the immigrants reflected a city's particular migration history. So, in Boston those gardeners who were immigrants came from Great Britain, Ireland, Italy, Germany, Canada, Russia, and Switzerland. Like the other cities, too, "few had had previous experience at farm work," and most "had to be taught every detail from the planting to the harvesting of the crops."[38] In any event, the gardens were a success. After a season of doping up the potato plants with Paris Green (a commonly used chemical of the era, a mixture of trioxide of arsenic and copper acetate) to fight off the beetles and the blight, the gardeners harvested 20 to 55 bushels of potatoes per plot. Paris Green is now known to be too toxic to human beings for safe agricultural use.[39]

The Industrial Aid Society's experiment at Morton Farm continued two more years, during 1896 and 1897, despite mounting losses caused by a potato blight that was then sweeping through New England. Many of the gardeners continued from year to year, and the number of applications rose to one hundred. The project, however, was terminated after 1897 for want of fresh land. The Vacant Lots Committee had hoped to secure land from the Boston Park Department, but the commissioners of that day, then aggressively expanding their chain of public open lands, must have believed that vegetable gardening by poor people was not a suitable sport to add to their facilities for tennis, golf, cricket, baseball, bowling, skating, and swimming.[40] In 1898 the Industrial Aid Society reaffirmed its belief in such charity gardens, but it was unable to find the necessary land at a price it considered reasonable.[41] Boston's small experiment with allotment gardens then died, not from the Colorado beetle but from lack of imagination.

Control of land has always been the rock that smashed American urban garden projects. Even though gardeners might organize for mutual aid, unless they could get a lease or title to their plots, the land would soon be taken from them. And how could an organization of low-income families lease or purchase expensive city land? A ten-year Chicago experiment with these early potato gardens tells the story directly. Here a gardeners' organization advanced further toward self-help than the members of any other contemporary community garden, but in the end their garden was destroyed by the philanthropic patrons.

In the spring of 1897, in imitation of other cities, Chicago's private philanthropic agency, the Bureau of Associated Charities, plowed up a forty-acre tract on the southwest side of the city (Englewood) and parceled out one-quarter-acre lots to 148 families. The Cook County Board of Commissioners appropriated $500 for seed. That first season the gardeners, who were native and immigrant, black and white, formed a "People's Friendly Club" to give mutual aid and to deal with the garden supervisor who had been appointed by the Associated Charities.[42] A brief abstract of one meeting of the gardeners has been printed. It consisted of crop reports and an appeal for more cooperation among the gardeners in tending each others' plots, and it concluded with the appointment of a committee to supervise the parceling out of the allotments for the next season.[43]

The program lasted for ten years with over two hundred families participating each year.[44] The philanthropists regarded the gardens as an exemplary bit of encouragement to the poor. In a typical report they wrote, "It is safe to say that the money return was considerably larger than the total money expenditure, while the return in the way of healthful and stimulating employment and in preventing poor families from going upon the charity lists was itself ample to justify the continuance of the gardens."[45]

Despite the fact that the gardeners paid fees sufficient to cover the costs of the plowing and harrowing, and despite the popularity of the two forty-acre "farms" that Associated Charities had established, the philanthropists lost interest and the poor lost their gardens.[46] City beautification replaced self-help as a charity enthusiasm. First Chicago's South Park Commission seized part of one of the gardens to make it into a public park;[47] then the philanthropists turned their attention to planting trees and ornamenting vacant lots, thereby closing out their vegetable garden program.[48]

The idea of a city that would provide open spaces to those who wished to garden was a concept quite beyond the American imagination. A poor man might enjoy a walk in the new public parks which were being laid out in cities across the nation, and his son might even be furnished with a baseball diamond for his games, but voters, politicians, and philanthropists all agreed that it would be wrong for a poor father or mother to have some claim on a small plot of city land for raising vegetables. Free land and homesteads were farm policies, while yards and open ground in the city were facilities for the well-settled and the prosperous only.

War Gardens

The food shortages of World War I exposed the folly of people who reckoned their town to be a city because it was all built up, or who saw in every vacant lot a chance to raise up another building. The massive drafts of men into armies, the blockades of food shipments, and the destruction of crops and farmland during the fighting caused severe food shortages across Europe. To cope with rationing and high prices, city dwellers planted thousands of community gardens in the vacant open spaces of their cities. In England 1,300,000 urban gardeners saved their nation from malnutrition, if not starvation, during the submarine blockade. The fact that they could accomplish so much, and so quickly, led some observers to speculate about peacetime problems and possibilities. An English author surmised that high prices for city foodstuffs resulted from monopoly practices: the inability of urban gardeners to get long-term access to land and the collusion of railroads and wholesalers to control city market prices.[49]

No less startling than the huge volume of output was the sudden wartime elevation of the social standing of urban gardeners. Formerly thought of as poor people in want of food and instruction, they became full-fledged, patriotic citizens. The leader of the United States campaign for war gardens imagined the gardeners to be people who, unable to serve in the army, wanted to "take an active part in some effort which would show tangible results in the struggle for right and justice."[50]

In the United States the planting of urban war gardens during 1917, 1918, and 1919 went forward in a climate of patriotic slogans put forth by a national organization set up for the very purpose. The National War Garden Committee, an affiliate of the American Forestry Association, issued press releases and posters to encourage people to grow vegetables—"Every Garden a Munitions Plant," "Sow the Seeds of Victory," "War Gardens Over the Top," "Slacker Land," "The Kaiser Is Canned." The leader of this organization, Charles Lathrop Pack (1857–1937), was a wealthy lumberman from Cleveland, Ohio, an advocate and promoter of scientific forestry and national resource conservation. President of the American Forestry Association from 1916 to 1922, Pack used his position to establish a national campaign for home food production. As in Europe, the effort was successful. In 1918 an estimated 5 million gardeners produced $520,000,000 worth of food, thereby releasing American farm supplies for shipment overseas.[51]

Exact records of Boston's participation do not survive, but it was estimated in 1919 that three thousand Bostonians were at work in gardens during 1918. The Park Department even loaned some of its land, plowing up a section of Franklin Park in Dorchester, and it also offered plots elsewhere. The downtown Women's City Club set out a very elaborate demonstration garden on the baseball fields at the southwest corner of Boston Common (at Charles and Boylston streets), where they grew thirty-five varieties of vegetables, everything then imaginable except corn.[52]

Pack's 1919 review of this wartime effort casts an informative light upon our present community gardens. He, like the gardeners of today, knew nothing of the history of previous gardens, and he, like so many garden promoters, was quite unaware of the political consequences of his proposals. Therefore, he repeated the past: yet one more time the established and the powerful of a city were to organize the gardeners: yet one more time the gardeners were not able to organize themselves or to achieve their own ends.

We owe the popular label "victory garden" to Pack and his organization. He used it after the armistice to urge people to continue their war gardens as victory gardens so that the food supplies of the United States could be supplemented and more food made available for the starving peoples of Europe and Russia.[53] The term became the promotional slogan for gardens during World War II and it has continued as a popular American name for allotment gardens ever since.

Pack also made an attack on vacant urban land, but his was strictly a wartime campaign and therefore the overtones of his reasoning did not carry on into years of peace. In order to encourage or embarrass owners of vacant land into lending it to gardeners, Pack's campaign called vacant lots "slacker land," land not contributing to the war effort. By his estimate there were at least fifty acres of tillable land in every city.[54]

In seeking the land, and especially in proposing large community gardens of many plots, Pack proposed the sort of top-down civic campaign that was commonplace in his era and that continues today in the form of United Fund campaigns and many city-wide charitable drives. He did not conceive of giving the gardeners themselves any voice, or of seeking out their interests.[55] Since no one consulted any of the gardeners' wishes, all their land eventually reverted to its former uses. Yet both the European examples and the wartime experience did linger in the back of people's minds as precedents to be called forth in exceptional circumstances.

For example, in 1922 the Boston-based city planner John Nolen (1869–1937) was commissioned to design a model industrial suburb for Cincinnati, Ohio. Because Nolen was an admirer of English town planning, his Mariemont scheme called for the provision of three sets of allotment gardens for resident working-class families.[56] During the Great Depression of the 1930s a number of cities in the United States, and a number of railroad and industrial corporations, established "relief gardens," temporary potato patches that repeated the experiments of the 1890s. There is no record that the City of Boston undertook such a program, although it is probable that individual landowners let poor people make gardens on some unused land. In New York City the welfare department, aided by the federal Works Progress Administration, ran an ambitious vacant lot garden project of five thousand gardens. In 1937, however, the program had to be closed because support for urban vegetable gardening conflicted with the Department of Agriculture's new idea—a food stamp distribution of surplus farm products.[57]

The New Deal also experimented with a very ambitious "subsistence homestead" program for urban industrial workers. On the fringes of Chicago, Wilmington, and Los Angeles it built small houses on one- to three-acre lots that were themselves planted with fruit trees and vegetables. The hope was that by part-time gardening workers and their families could supplement their incomes and thereby attain a decent standard of living and adequate financial security. At the time of the 1935 report 22,000 people had applied for 5,000 proposed homesteads.[58]

When World War II came, many recalled the gardens of the First World War. During the peak year, 1944, 20 million victory gardeners produced 44 percent of the fresh vegetables in the United States. In Boston the *Boston Globe*, the Advertising Club, the School Department, and the Department of Parks and Recreation sponsored a Victory Garden Committee and its activities. The Boston Common was plowed and planted once more, and a number of industrial firms loaned land near their plants. The Parks Department plowed up forty-nine sites around the city, and the School Department undertook to give horticultural instruction to any who wished it. An estimated 2,600 families grew vegetables in these wartime gardens. Since all the sites were mere loans, all the victory gardens disappeared with the armistice except one, the Fenway Victory Gardens.[59]

The Fenway gardens were established on seven and a half acres of Parks Department land in the spring of 1942. The plots averaged 15 × 25 feet, a size typical of the small American allotment. Today there are four hundred active gardeners. In the late fall of 1944 the Fenway group set themselves up as a formal club, the Fenway Garden Society. The society elects a superintendent who parcels out the plots and is responsible to the Commissioner of Parks and Recreation of the City of Boston. Any resident of the city may apply for space and, if there is an opening, may garden for a season upon payment of a small annual fee. The revenues from the annual dues go to maintain an elaborate water system. By the judicious courting of politicians the Fenway Garden Society has been able to continue its free use of its park land from World War II to the present.

On several occasions the gardens were threatened by proposals for alternative uses for the land. At one moment a candidate for the state senate, John J. Moakley of South Boston, proposed that the garden land be paved over for a parking lot to serve the baseball patrons of nearby Fenway Park. At that time one of the active Fenway gardeners was Senator John E. Powers, also of South Boston, a man who had promised, when he ran for mayor of Boston in 1955, that he would turn every vacant lot in the city into a garden. Senator Powers defeated Representative Moakley's bill by tabling it on its second reading when it came up to the senate. This fortunate convergence of a strong gardeners' organization with political support saved the Fenway gardens, and, indeed, it foreshadowed a new era in urban community gardening that would begin in various city neighborhoods across the United States some time between Earth Day, 22 April 1970, and the summer of 1975 when the U.S. Department of Agriculture began its Food and Nutrition Education experiment.[60]

New Garden Politics

Today's American urban community garden is the child of new politics and abandoned city land. The new politics arose out of the Afro-American civil rights movement of the 1960s. The vacant lots came from the emptying out of the centers of American cities when they were rebuilt in their current low-density suburban-metropolitan forms.[61] Together the empowerment of new politics and the opportunities of vacant land have created a historically unprecedented series of class and racial coalitions—organizations of blacks and whites, poor and well-to-do, longtime city residents and newcomers from the suburbs. These new coalitions bring urban neighbors together to plant and maintain community gardens, to manage neighborhood land, and to set fresh goals for the rebuilding of the American city.

The prime force in the new garden politics comes from the cooperation of black and white community leaders. On the Afro-American side the slow but steady advance of civil rights that began with the discrediting of racism by World War II brought forward a group of men and women who were effective advocates of the politics of dignity and self-help. Some received their training in civil rights organizations like the NAACP and the Urban League. More gained experience in a variety of city organizations and committees concerned with nutrition, child care, schools, juvenile delinquency, and housing. During the sixties many federal programs required the formation of local boards as part of their mode of operation. As a consequence of all these changes new voices were heard in City Hall as well as next door.[62]

The first activists on the white side of the community gardening coalitions were recruited by a thousand frustrations and political disagreements with the directions in which the United States was being led during the sixties and early seventies. A short list might include the Vietnam War, atomic bomb testing, environmental pollution, U.S. food gluts amidst domestic malnutrition and starvation overseas, the Arab oil embargo, and, like their Afro-American partners, the civil rights campaigns and their conflicts with established municipal politics. The pioneer community organizers were Peace Corps graduates, antiwar activists, out-of-work architects and landscape professionals. All had been drawn by one cause or another into living in the inner city at the very moment when most of their fellows were heading for the suburbs. Once settled in the city, they confronted the tensions between the opportunities for rebuilding that the abandoned land offered and a series of practices and policies that attacked inner-city residents.[63]

A slow transition that advanced through many different programs carried the nation from its old habits of intermittent philanthropy to a position of responding to the needs expressed by the gardeners themselves. It took ten to fifteen years for the new approach to receive widespread attention. Since there was no national organization of community gardeners in 1960, no national history of the transition survives. Today's garden activists, however, recall a sequence of events that they say began with public housing gardens, then shifted to the provision of community open spaces and gardens in new suburban subdivisions, and finally turned to projects that sought neighborhood approval, construction, and maintenance for inner city open spaces.

In Virginia the Norfolk Housing Authority seems to have been the national pioneer in organizing its tenants into garden clubs and in awarding prizes for the best flowerbeds. During World War II Cleveland followed Norfolk's example but, of course, emphasized vegetable growing. In Seattle the local district federation of garden clubs initiated a gardening program for public housing tenants. In 1958 the Chicago Housing Authority commenced an annual contest for the "most beautiful housing project in Chicago" in an attempt to stimulate its maintenance employees and to reduce tenant littering and vandalism.[64]

In 1963 the New York City Housing Authority imitated the Chicago program but transformed it into a competition among tenant flower gardeners. Under the New York rules the tenants had to form themselves into groups. The groups might be composed of either children or adults. Each spring the groups apply for gardening space and thereafter they are given free lectures by experts, a gardening book, and free seeds. In mid-August the flower beds are judged and prizes awarded. In none of these cases—Norfolk, Chicago, New York, or elsewhere—was there any evidence that the gardens emerged from tenant initiatives. The housing authority gardens, however, have been very popular, and tenants have returned to their same plots year after year.[65]

The victory gardens of Davis, California, proved very influential for suburban subdivision design. They continued as community gardens after the war, setting an example for the layout of several new subdivisions that reserved common land for community garden space. Because Davis was the location of the School of Agriculture of the University of California, its precedents traveled quickly around the country and joined other experimental designs for common land in suburban layouts.[66]

In 1961 the city of Philadelphia, then nationally prominent for its ambitious urban renewal program, decided to get control of its tax-delinquent parcels, in part to keep them from becoming nuisances, and in part to use them to establish a land bank for later public use and development. The next year the city hired a social worker, Eve Asner, to begin a program of small park development using such lots. Aided by a U.S. Housing and Urban Development beautification grant, she built sixty small parks and play spaces during the years 1965–67. The most significant aspect of Asner's program was not its many cleaned-up public spaces, desirable though they were, but her use of the new political outlook. As she reported later, "A project is begun only at the request of a neighborhood group, and residents are required to participate in planning and construction, and to assume total responsibility for maintenance."[67]

This approach fostered a new outlook upon public parks and playgrounds. A distinction began to be drawn between nineteenth-century–style parks that the municipal authorities attempted to maintain, and land that nearby residents continually refashioned. In 1966 Robin Moore's Lenox-Camden Playground in Boston's lower Roxbury section attracted a lot of professional attention as another example of the new approach. Here, on a junk-filled lot between two housing projects, he led a team of local children and adults in the construction of a playground. Construction mixed play with building: the goal was making activity spaces, not a finished installation.[68]

The basic shift in the political situation of community gardening, however, came only when the general public adopted an outlook of self-help. Ordinary city dwellers and landless suburbanites stopped waiting for public institutions to provide land for them and began, instead, to demand land and services from their municipalities. This tidal change took place sometime between 1968 and 1976. The implications of that shift, and the emotions that propelled it, can be estimated by recalling the ten-year public drama over the so-called People's Park which opened in Berkeley, California, in 1969. At this writing the People's Park is still part parking lot, part university field, part straggly garden. Both the memory of its past and its present state serve as reminders of civic failure and frustration in the management of vacant lots.[69]

The ten years of confrontations represent a breakdown in local institutions' ability to share power. At the outset the empty lot became a symbol of public frustration with the prolonging of the Vietnam War. But the fact that a vacant lot could serve as such a lightning rod showed that beneath the moment's extreme tensions of war and race conflict the control of urban land by big institutions had become an important citizen grievance. The muddy, car-filled lot, the chain-link fence, the paved parking spaces, all stood in opposition to the public desire to use city land directly—to gather together, to party, to make noise, to debate, and to garden. Such informal and personal land uses were the very antitheses of war, interstate highways, and urban renewal land takings.

While Berkeley offered its continuing People's Park drama, cities across the nation faced the problems of more and more abandoned lots, more and more trash-filled and rat-infested eyesores. Abandoned land became a symbol of the American city's inability to keep its own house in order. In New York City, the center of the United States' television and newspaper attention, Mayor John Lindsay launched an ambitious "vest-pocket park" program in an attempt to combat the evil. Many lots were cleared of rubble, paved, and given play equipment, but since the program was not based on prior neighborhood consultation and response it soon fell victim to vandals.[70]

By 1972 local initiatives stemming from the new garden outlook began to multiply rapidly. In that year the mayor of Syracuse, N.Y., began his "adopt-a-lot" scheme whereby he encouraged local residents to garden on abandoned property. In Boston, at the outer edge of the city, a group began a community garden on the grounds of a little-used state mental hospital. Ironically, their site was very close to the charity potato fields of 1895. In Burlington, Vermont, B. H. Thompson laid out a community garden that soon became the nursery of an important national gardening organization. And in New York City a group of landscape professionals set up an informal organization, the Green Guerrillas, to give assistance to people who wanted to start gardens in vacant lots. By 1975 the Green Guerrillas had 35 members and a big corps of volunteers, and they had succeeded in capturing public attention and sympathy. That same year the New York Botanic Garden called together a conference of experts from a number of American cities to discuss urban gardening technique. These meetings gave professional legitimacy to a movement that had been, until then, a scattered series of independent initiatives.[71]

Suddenly, in the spring and summer of 1976, all across the nation, community groups organized and started new community vegetable and flower gardens. That same summer the U.S. Department of Agriculture, encouraged by Congressman Frederick Richmond of Brooklyn, N.Y., started an experiment in New York City. Congressman Richmond had been president of the New York Urban League from 1959 to 1964, and New York City Human Rights Commissioner from 1964 to 1970. In this experiment the USDA employed its extension staff to train inner-city citizens in the arts of vacant lot vegetable gardening. Two years later, in 1978, the organizers of community gardens from many American cities came together in Chicago to meet each other for the first time, to compare experiences, and to form a national organization, the American Community Garden Association.[72]

The New Politics in Boston

The postwar changes in the American city traced patterns in Boston similar to many others. First came the suburban exodus, then the taking up of old neighborhoods by Afro-Americans and Hispanics. The newcomers, however, were too few to replace the emigrants: rents fell, landlords abandoned their properties, tax revenues failed to keep pace with rising costs, and municipal services were cut back and compromised. The decline in the public quality of the inner city went forward at the same moment as expectations for comfort and services in the suburban metropolis bounded upward. The city then countered with ambitious urban renewal projects which themselves carried off still more buildings, and the federal government added its gigantic highway clearances. Out of the frustrations and conflicts of these massive changes there emerged a new politics of land and the new community gardening.

Because it was a small and densely packed city that was surrounded by vast tracts of open suburban land, Boston underwent three decades of massive population transfers. Thousands of resident families took up houses in the suburbs, and their places were taken by a much smaller immigration of Afro-Americans from other United States cities and from the South Atlantic states, by small communities of Hispanics, particularly from Puerto Rico and the Caribbean, and by small numbers of Asians from China, Vietnam, and Cambodia.

In 1950 the city of Boston held 801,444 inhabitants, of whom 5 percent were black and a very few Hispanic or Chinese. By 1980 the city showed a net loss of 30 percent of its population. Of the 563,000 who remained, 20 percent were Afro-Americans, 3 to 5 percent were Hispanic, and 3 percent were Oriental.[73]

These population shifts sharply reduced the density of the old, inner working-class sections of the city: Charlestown, East Boston, West End, South End, and Roxbury. Low rents in these sections attracted new settlers, but low rents and low incomes also brought extensive landlord abandonment. Abandonment, failing tax collections, arson, and cheap properties turned these areas into municipal real estate liabilities, and once they became real estate problems they became targets for Boston's urban renewal and highway clearance.

Soon after the passage of federal urban renewal legislation, the Boston City Planning Board proposed what was, in the 1950s, a typical plan: it recommended clearing eleven hundred acres of inner-city land of its existing structures. Accordingly, the entire West End was flattened and, beginning in 1958, replaced with expensive apartment towers. The callousness of this West End project, the city's first major undertaking, the ignoring of the West End residents, the excessive clearance, and the sudden replacement of low- and moderate-income families by the well-to-do was shocking.[74]

In 1960 a new mayor, John F. Collins, imported a fresh administrator, Edward J. Logue, from New Haven, Connecticut, to direct a very extensive series of urban renewal projects for the city. Logue had been relatively responsive to local groups in his New Haven renewal work, and he set up a social planning agency, Action for Boston Community Development.[75] His administration inaugurated two decades of neighborhood bargaining and neighborhood defense, which to this day are a prominent feature of the city's politics.

Among the innumerable conflicts of the ensuing years, the 1968 "Tent City" protests of a coalition of black and white South End residents stands out because of the clarity of its issues. In the course of carrying out its renewal plans, the Boston Redevelopment Authority tore down a block of houses that were home to a hundred poor families. At that time the authority had not built any nearby low-rent housing suitable for the residents it displaced. Instead, it leased the cleared Dartmouth Street lot to a parking operator who catered to nearby office workers. The neighborhood activists, drawn together in an ad hoc group named CAUSE (Community Assembly for a United South End), regarded this transfer as the last straw in a series of similar events. They staged a sit-in at the local Redevelopment Authority offices. However, the all-day Thursday, 25 April, sit-in failed to attract public notice, so the group attempted on Friday to block off the parking lot itself. The ensuing traffic jam brought police, police brought arrests, and arrests brought lots of reporters and cameramen. On Sunday CAUSE set up tents and occupied the lot once more. This time their presence brought the promise of more regular neighborhood consultation, and some time later the Boston Redevelopment Authority established an elected South End Project Area Committee (SEPAC). At this writing housing is at last being built on the Tent City lot.[76]

Such neighborhood militancy in Boston and other cities did slowly influence federal legislation and guidelines, and it did alter local land and housing bargains. In a few cases Boston urban renewal projects became models of community participation and design. Particularly notable were the designs of architect John Sharratt: Villa Victoria (1968–76) for a Hispanic group in the South End; Madison Park (1967–80) cluster housing for an Afro-American coalition in Roxbury; and Mission Park (1969–76) for a racially mixed organization near the Harvard University hospitals in Roxbury.[77]

Community organization for urban renewal participation and defense merged easily with highway politics. By 1967, through expanding existing road and railway alignments, Massachusetts had completed large segments of its metropolitan interstate highway system. Standard American designs of those years called for constructing a metropolitan spiderweb of freeways, radials from the center city, and two or more circumferentials running around the metropolis. In Boston the program called for adding an inner belt route to the already built outer Route 128 and the contemplated distant Route 495.

The inner belt had to traverse densely built old residential sections. Moreover, since it would connect all the radial highways, it required giant multi-level interchanges. Highway planners designed an elevated highway which would be built on top of cleared land in the Charlestown, East Boston, Roxbury, and Jamaica Plain sections of Boston and in the adjacent cities of Cambridge and Somerville. A group of academics, city activists, and Cambridge politicians began the opposition when the highway authorizations and clearances were announced in 1967 and 1968. Soon they were joined by Mayor Kevin

White of Boston and his staff, and by a group of volunteer city planners and neighborhood organizers who contacted groups in Roxbury and Jamaica Plain. The coalition finally succeeded in persuading Governor Francis Sargent to call off construction in February 1970, and later to request, successfully, that U.S. Highway Trust funds be made available for public transit construction. This anti-highway coalition stopped the building of much of the proposed elevated highway, but not before an eight-and-a-half mile strip of land had been cleared of homes and businesses. A good deal of the former highway-designated land in the Southwest Corridor of Jamaica Plain and Roxbury stands vacant to this day.[78]

Although housing abandonment, arson, urban renewal, and highways had cleared several thousand acres of inner-city land, it took the leadership and experiences of the civil rights campaigns to transform the rubble-strewn lots into community gardens. In Boston civil rights conflicts took on a particularly bitter quality because the Afro-American community was relatively small and politically under-represented. Also, it was opposed by a group of white politicians who saw that their self-interest lay in encouraging white racism and in maintaining their own control of a segregated public school system and its patronage. In addition, unlike other cities where business and union leadership joined to support civil rights, Boston leaders remained apathetic or even hostile to Afro-American demands.

Boston's particular civil rights campaign had begun in 1963 when a group of residents requested an interview with the Boston School Committee to discuss the inadequate education that was then being offered to their children. School Committee Chairperson Louise Day Hicks rebuffed the request and subsequently led an extended campaign against reform and accommodation. In June 1963 eight thousand schoolchildren boycotted the Boston public schools.[79]

Next, the local NAACP filed a lawsuit requesting that the City of Boston cease operating segregated public schools, and the case then dragged through the federal courts. Hearings, investigations, protests, and marches ensued. The same sorts of rising frustrations and brief rebellions seized Boston as other American cities.[80]

On Friday, 2 June 1967, while Senators Robert and Edward Kennedy conducted day-long hearings on the adequacy of federal social legislation downtown at Faneuil Hall, at Grove Hall, in the Afro-American section of Roxbury, a women's welfare rights organization, Mothers for Adequate Welfare, occupied the offices of the local welfare office. The women of this organization had been protesting welfare policies and practices for five years, and they hoped that the presence of the senators might attract attention and sympathy for their cause. Their platform particularly objected to the current practice that paid too few benefits to support a family and simultaneously forbade recipients' working to supplement their income. The sit-in brought out a large contingent of nervous white policemen, and the policemen's presence, in turn, attracted a large black crowd. As the afternoon wore on, the police and the crowd multiplied until at 5:15, when the police broke into the welfare offices and started to drag out the protesters, the crowd attacked the police with fists and stones. A long evening of police and neighborhood violence followed. And the next two nights brought more fighting and harassment, until on Sunday night the heavily armed and much hated tactical police force was withdrawn from the ghetto.[81]

Violence moved into some of the white quarters of Boston in 1974 when a U.S. District Court judge ordered white and black children to be driven back and forth across the city to establish racially mixed classrooms. South Boston and Charlestown attempted violent opposition, while elsewhere in the city there were nasty racial incidents, racial attacks, house bombings, and even racial murders.[82] Neither the federal judge nor the elected school committee was able to establish a satisfactory multi-racial public school system. At the same time the rebuilding of the central city under urban renewal did not soften the iron divisions between ill-paying and well-paying jobs. Forty-four percent of Boston's population, black and white, continued to live at the lowest income level, or below the poverty line, and predictions foretold a worsening future. Faced with such bitter racial conflict and such a failure of community effort to relieve the economic injustices of the city, one quarter of the white population of Boston fled the city during the decade from 1970 to 1980. Most were families with school-age children.[83]

In such a political maelstrom the two thousand-odd acres of cleared and abandoned city land stood as open wounds reminding the passerby of Boston's defeat. Yet, for a few citizens the land nobody wanted offered a fresh opportunity. As in other cities the most immediate opportunity lay in gardening, turning the nearby ugly and often dangerous lots into a source of family food and personal accomplishment.

The gardening responses themselves drew from both political traditions: sometimes from the new politics of neighborhood self-determination, sometimes from the tradition of public philanthropy. Today's community gardeners recall that in the early 1970s people began gardening on lots adjacent to their homes without formal organization or formal permission.[84] Only on those few lots that were not buried with rubble and contractors' trash, or stripped of topsoil by bulldozers, could such small beginnings advance. Already in 1970, however, the people living next to Cedar Square in Roxbury Highlands had taken up gardening on a vacant lot, and some years later this success carried them forward to build a "survival garden," as they called it, nearby on Linwood Street.[85]

Across Roxbury, in the Grove Hall section, Mrs. Augusta Bailey of 73 Wayne Street had for years been running an old-fashioned beautification program, but with the impoverishment of her neighborhood she had, in addition, turned to teaching nutrition to poor families and to feeding children in a housing project. In this work she was aided by a youth worker and community organizer from suburban Weston, William McElwain. Mr.

McElwain had established his Green Power Farm in 1970 as part of a youth program for Weston young people, but he had worked in the South End and he wanted to use food to help establish a new politics and new social relations. He sold his vegetables to food cooperatives and gave food to Mrs. Bailey. Both shared the idea that poor families should be able to get access to land so that they could raise their own food if they wished to.[86]

The first formal public step toward a new politics of community gardening came with the election of Melvin H. King to the state legislature in 1972. Representative King was a former director of the Eastern Massachusetts Urban League and had tried repeatedly to get elected to a seat on the Boston School Committee in 1961, 1963, and 1965. An advocate of black nationalism and a man who was deeply committed to the issue of local control of land, he had been a leader in the Tent City action of 1968 and was a severe critic of top-down planning. In 1971 he joined the Massachusetts Institute of Technology faculty as an adjunct professor to assist its Department of Urban Studies and Planning with its community fellows program. As a state representative Mr. King successfully sponsored the Massachusetts Gardening and Farm Act of 1974, legislation which stated that gardeners and farmers might use vacant public land at no cost. As has always been the custom in the United States, however, the use of the land was subject to termination on short notice.[87]

Such legislation might give permission to some, but it could not build urban gardens. Two-thirds of Boston's vacant parcels were held by private owners, and, public or private, most were unsuitable for cultivation because of insufficient soil or pollution by lead and other poisons. In most parts of the city making a new urban garden required sustained effort to clean up the lot, to find fresh topsoil, to secure water, and to enclose the garden. Representative King's Gardening and Farm Act did at least remove some legal barriers, and it evoked some sensible public recognition to the embarrassing absurdity of the city's vacant lots.

During the winter of 1976 Mayor Kevin White's administration decided to allocate some of the federal government's new Community Development Block Grant funds to a gardening program. For the first year the city earmarked $500,000 for twenty gardens whose combined acreage came to a little less than six acres. Seeking quick success for its "Revival Gardens," as it named them, it urged some existing community gardens to join the municipal effort, and it organized a few new gardens. Fresh soil, mulch, fencing, water, shrubs, and trees were promised, but the city's project better served its contractors than its gardeners. The contractors did not deliver on time for the planting season, and often their materials proved inferior. Moreover, the Revival Gardens offered the enrolled gardeners neither control over the program nor leases or other security of tenure for their gardens.[88]

While the Revival Gardens went forward, the Boston Redevelopment Authority launched an Open Space Management effort which continued from 1977 through 1981. The city spent $2,266,000 to clean up 178 acres of land it owned.[89] But the same defects that plagued the Revival Garden effort handicapped this cleanup. The work was expensive ($83,000 per acre for Revival Gardens, $12,722 per acre for Open Space Management), contractors were unreliable, and the cleaned lot was not usually a piece of land lending itself to community-affirming use.

These public vacant lot programs stimulated the same sort of responses as urban renewal and New York City's vest-pocket parks: local residents felt left out of the planning and were often not pleased with what have been given to them. Immediately after the Revival Gardens had been announced, the proponents of the new politics in community gardening began to organize. In April 1976 Augusta Bailey organized a one-day conference on the inner city environment.

The active participants of this first conference represented in their persons many of the streams of experience and outlook that were then converging in cities across the United States: Representative King was a civil rights leader, youth worker, and community organizer; Augusta Bailey was an old-style beautification advocate who had turned her attention to poverty and nutrition; William McElwain was a former school teacher and farmer who was organizing young people around the politics of food; Morell Baber was a Mississippi migrant to Boston, a welfare mother, and a member of the South End Project Area Committee; Charlotte Kahn, also of SEPAC, was a resident of the South End who had planted a garden for children in her neighborhood; and Mark Anderson was a former upstate New York farmer who was then working as activities director for the Salvation Army's Harbor Light Center in the South End. They were joined at their first conference by the Green Guerrillas, veterans of the garden campaigns of New York.

Some weeks later Representative King called a meeting of residents of the South End and lower Roxbury who were interested in organizing community gardens. With the help of his legislative aide, Judith Wagner, he located 3,000 square yards of topsoil, which belonged to the Metropolitan District Commission. It was, however, located in Marlborough, twenty-five miles from Boston. Charlotte Kahn then persuaded the National Guard to truck the dirt into the city, while Mark Anderson and his Harbor Light group stayed up all night making meatballs and sauce to serve the Guardsmen spaghetti dinners the next day. Six gardens were established that summer. Indeed, one of them was on Columbus Avenue in Lower Roxbury, very near the site of Boston's first school garden of 1891. In addition, through SEPAC, the group secured a small grant to hire a full-time gardener and two carpenters to help local residents fence and begin tending the many plots at the gardens.[90]

Despite the lateness of the season a passable crop was planted and harvested. Volunteer organizers worked very hard that first summer and the following spring securing more sites, organizing neighborhood gardeners, finding water and fencing for the plots, and looking for more soil and mulch. They began calling themselves Boston Urban Gardeners. By the summer of 1977 the core group of the South End Garden Project had enlisted the support and cooperation of many groups interested in community gardens: Edward L. Cooper and John Ellertson of the Highland Park gardens, garden groups in Jamaica Plain, Dorchester, and Brighton, and the staffs of Action for Boston Community Development and the Massachusetts Department of Food and Agriculture. In August 1977 they incorporated as a permanent nonprofit organization with Judith Wagner and Charlotte Kahn serving as volunteer co-directors. Boston Urban Gardeners is an umbrella organization designed to facilitate the activities of city gardeners and to enlarge their voice in Boston and Massachusetts politics.

The Boston Urban Gardeners' Coalitions

Except for the occasional garden that is started by a resident on a lot adjacent to his or her home, community gardens come into being only through processes that embrace both neighborhood and city-wide politics. The costs of land preparation, especially in lead-contaminated Boston soils, exceed the resources of most garden groups, so that public funds must be found and alliances must be made if a workable set of plots is to be secured. Once the sites are cleared and the new soil furnished, the community gardeners can care for themselves. To understand the political dynamics of community gardening, it is useful to review two cases, the Highland Park 400 Survival Garden of Roxbury, and the Southwest Corridor Community Farm of Jamaica Plain. The first is the lengthened shadow of one man, Edward L. Cooper, a longtime community activist who devoted several years to establishing this garden in his neighborhood. It is now a handsome garden where the elderly can grow their own vegetables. The second project is located on land once cleared for an interstate highway. Here the gardeners operate a greenhouse to grow plants for Boston's community gardens, train urban gardeners, and provide some neighborhood plots.[91]

In 1975, when the oil crisis and rising farm prices combined to confront low-income Americans with stark "heat or eat" alternatives, Edward Cooper organized the Highland Park 400 Survival Garden in Roxbury. The "400" represented the number of senior citizens in this predominantly black neighborhood in the first natural rise of land about two and a half miles south of downtown Boston.

Once the location of prosperous summer mansions overlooking the waters of the now-filled Back Bay and Fens, the neighborhood had been gradually developed until, with the advent of mass transit at the end of the nineteenth century, it rapidly joined the era of the streetcar suburbs of Boston. Since then, following the slow decline of Boston's industrial economy and the devastating exodus to the suburbs following World War II, the neighborhood first lost population and then lost its structures to insurance and bank redlining, landlord disinvestment, arson, abandonment, and demolition.

The garden itself sits at the top of Highland Park on ground that once contained three houses. The neighborhood still reflects its varied architectural past: colonial era farmhouses and mansions share the streetscape with later mansard-roofed, wooden, worker housing and attached brick townhouses. Everywhere the neighborhood is dotted with vacant lots, quite a few of which have been transformed into household and community gardens by new residents who learned how to grow vegetables in the rural American South and the Caribbean, or by younger residents eager to create a healthy environment in which to raise their families.

The Highland Park 400 Survival Garden was the first of the community gardens in this part of Boston, and it remains one of the finest in the city. The former director of both the Urban League and the NAACP in Boston, and retired project manager for the Boston Redevelopment Authority, Edward Cooper used the garden to organize black senior citizens—his neighbors—who were suffering from poverty, lack of exercise, and the inaccessibility of affordable fresh produce and other foods. The neighborhood had been abandoned by a supermarket chain some years earlier: it was not a profitable location. In the spring of 1976 Cooper began single-handedly to purchase and to distribute eggs and meat in bulk from the wholesale markets to help his neighbors cut their food bills. He also applied to the City of Boston's Revival Program for assistance in constructing a community garden.

The Revival Program was funded with federal Community Development Block Grant moneys, administered by the Department of Housing and Urban Development. Designed to fund major capital improvement projects in blighted urban areas, the funds carried with them requirements for closed bids, union-scale wages, and other regulations that prolonged the length of projects and created confusion and a sense of helplessness on the part of local participants. Accordingly, once construction finally was underway, Ed Cooper began to look for additional allies and support.

In December of 1976 garden organizers from four Boston neighborhoods met to discuss common frustrations and plans and to share resources. At first the talk centered on practical issues such as the availability of seeds and tools. Very quickly, however, the conversation turned to the need to join forces to negotiate with the City of Boston about delays and confusion in the Revival Program. By the end of the meeting the five people present, including Ed Cooper, had decided to establish a city-wide gardening organization—Boston Urban Gardeners.

The first newsletter of the fledgling group was photocopied on two sides of an 8½ × 11-inch page:

ANNOUNCING! THE FORMATION OF BOSTON URBAN GARDENERS

The Boston Urban Gardeners was created last December 6th by a group of people who have been active in community gardening projects such as the South End Garden Project and the City's REVIVAL Victory Gardening program. We believe that a coalition of resident gardeners from every section of the city can work together to improve our existing gardens as well as introducing this creative activity to more and more Bostonians.

Even during this abnormally cold winter, we have been active and can point to some accomplishments: we have arranged for two large loads of Suffolk Downs manure to be dumped at two gardens, one in the South End and one in Roxbury; we submitted a draft evaluation of the REVIVAL Victory Garden program to the Little City Hall Managers to further inform their discussion in December of that program.

At the next meeting, at Ed Cooper's house, there were more gardeners. A host of urgent activities carried the Boston Urban Gardeners organization forward: deliveries of donated soil and horse manure, distribution of free seeds donated by the Department of Agriculture, and monitoring the city's Revival Program. By mid-spring there were weekly ad hoc Steering Committee meetings at which participants offered to the group the use of resources, several hours of trucking, fence supplies, perennials, and even, occasionally, real staff time or money. By scraping resources together and cementing them with the glue of determination, more gardens were created and existing gardens improved.

The Highland Park 400 Survival Garden, working from the base of new topsoil, fencing, and water supplied through the Revival Program, now had added about 120 yards of horse manure from the Suffolk Downs racetrack, a colorful display of annuals, and several fruit trees. The twenty-five senior citizens of Highland Park brought together by Ed Cooper were by now producing hundreds of pounds of fresh produce on a luxuriant hilltop site.

Beginning in 1979, Boston Urban Gardeners itself was funded in part by Community Development Block Grant funds of the federal government. With a grant of $90,000 Boston Urban Gardeners was able to work on thirty-eight individual garden sites at less than $2,000 per project, thereby circumventing the tangle of requirements that had undermined the Revival Garden Program. In 1979, therefore, Boston Urban Gardeners was able to support the Highland Park gardeners' requests for assistance with rototilling, garden expansion, and other tasks beyond the means of a senior citizens' garden group.

The garden itself began to be perceived as a solid element and symbol of hope in a community still subject to redlining and disinvestment. Yet as the residents improved their neighborhood, the threat to their garden increased. The land on which it sat was slated, according to the Boston Redevelopment Authority's initial plans, for new housing. Through the persuasive arguments of Ed Cooper, neighborhood leaders who were working for critically needed housing dollars nevertheless began to support preservation of the garden as a green oasis and as one symbol of a better future for the neighborhood.

In 1981 the 8,000-square-foot garden and an adjoining vacant parcel were purchased on behalf of the Highland Park 400 by the Boston Natural Areas Fund, a new ecology-minded organization dedicated to the preservation of green and open land in the city.

During the next few years (1982–84) Ed Cooper and Boston Urban Gardeners turned their attention to training young people for jobs in landscape contracting. The Highland Park garden served as one of the training grounds. The project went forward in two stages: first, the preparation of a formal garden design by professionals with the gardeners themselves as clients; and second, the in-training construction of the new design.

Anne Whiston Spirn's class in landscape architecture at the Harvard Graduate School of Design drew proposals for an expanded Highland Park garden. Drawings and models of each design were presented at an open and well-attended community meeting and were left on display for the next week, as gardeners and residents discussed their preferences, made notes on options, and informed neighbors of the second meeting.

The second gathering of the community produced an unexpected result. While the Harvard students had reserved a week to "mesh" the elements of various designs preferred by the community residents, the community quickly came to a full consensus for the designs of each site. Community members and gardeners suggested a few minor changes in the selected designs, and construction began the following day.

The construction was done as the "on-site" portion of Boston Urban Gardeners' recently initiated Landscape Skills Training Program, an activity funded with federal money through the city's Neighborhood Development and Employment Agency and held at Roxbury Community College. The twenty trainees worked with local landscape contractors and designers to upgrade the vegetable plots, install a new perennial garden and flower border, plant an *allée* of trees, install arbors for roses, and create a meadow for nursery plants. Ed Cooper's vision was to create a garden spot to rival the Boston Parks Department's Fenway Rose Garden. In his words:

> Open space is as much a part of urban design as zoning, buildings and streets. When I work, as I have, in the field of civil rights, and when I work, as I have, in the field of open space, it's always in the interest of making the overall community a better place to live. Our beautiful garden demonstrates a lot of things that blacks feel they can't do and whites feel can't be done in the black community. This garden serves as an inspiration to everybody of what is possible.

In August 1984 residents of the community and staff and board members of Boston Urban Gardeners, the Landscape Training Program trainees, staff from the Boston Natural Areas Fund, staff from the city's Neighborhood Development and Employment Agency, Anne Spirn, the students from the Harvard Graduate School of Design (including

Beth Arndtsen, whose design had been selected by the residents and who was subsequently hired as Boston Urban Gardeners' first staff landscape architect) gathered at the Highland Park site. The new rose and community gardens were rededicated as "Cooper's Place" in recognition of Edward L. Cooper's commitment to the community, his untiring dedication, and his aesthetic vision.

The very successes of the city's community gardeners threatened to undermine their existence. The positive effects of a community garden's social organization, the cooperation of neighbors, and the cleanup of the immediate neighborhood, transformed these vacant parcels into attractive sites for new construction. Only a few gardens like the large Fenway Victory Garden, which was sponsored by the Parks Department, or the still larger garden at the site of the former Boston State Mental Hospital, and Cooper's Place were secure. Most of the hundred-odd gardens around the city went forward without a title or lease. These gardens now occupy about twenty-five of the two thousand acres of vacant city lots. Although some agencies in the municipal government see the gardens as worthwhile additions to the city, old real estate policies still dominate City Hall thinking.

For example, in 1985 a long-standing and very successful small garden in Boston's South Cove was assigned to a syndicate of Chinese real estate developers. Ironically, these pocket-sized gardens had been some of the few places where Chinese immigrants and the American-born worked cooperatively together. Rather than preserve the garden and require the developers to select a site a few blocks farther from Boston's Chinatown, the municipal government now proposes to destroy this small bit of successful urban community life.

The South Cove case, following as it did similar actions in New York and other cities, brought forth yet another coalition for the defense of gardens and city open land. In August of 1985 several dozen Boston neighborhood organizations joined together with the Parks Department and some utilities and foundations to form an umbrella organization for the improvement of parks and open spaces in the city. Edward Cooper was elected to serve as the first president of the Boston Greenspace Alliance.[92]

The Southwest Corridor is a swath of land cleared during the mid-1960s for the proposed interstate highway I-95. The corridor runs through the low-income communities of Roxbury and cuts in two the residential valley streets between the rising uplands of Roxbury and Mission Hill on the one side and Jamaica Plain on the other. The issue symbolizes both the destructive power of large bureaucratic decisions and the counterforce of concerted community action. In 1968 a united five-community front succeeded in persuading Governor Francis Sargent to order a moratorium on highway construction within the area encompassed by metropolitan Boston's Route 128 circumferential road. Soon thereafter planning began for a massive development process, to begin with the relocation of Boston's turn-of-the-century elevated Orange Line rail transit to the Roxbury valley. As envisioned in the early 1970s, development would follow the relocated line and its adjacent commuter railroad so that one of the city's lowest-income areas might become the heart of the revitalization of the southern quarter of the city.

By the mid-1970s the land lay like a wide, unattended scar through neighborhoods reeling under the combined pressures of school busing, the energy crisis, and rapid downtown development and inner-city gentrification. The wide strip of land was being held by the City of Boston for future industrial and office development, but few purchasers or tenants could be attracted to these sites until the cheap land and old buildings close to the downtown had been taken up. While hundreds of thousands of hours had been expended by community residents at planning and design meetings conducted by public agencies, and as maps, charts, and models began to detail future projects, the bulldozed land itself was a barren reminder of former homes, businesses, and busy neighborhoods.

In the spring of 1976, when community gardens were sprouting on vacant land throughout the city, several longtime community leaders who had been living with the desolation and unfulfilled promise of the corridor for too many years decided to act. Mark Levine, director of Jamaica Plain's Ecumenical Social Action Committee, Lloyd King, director of the Roxbury Action Program, Charlotte Kahn and Mark Anderson of the South End Garden Project, and Jon Ellertson, a former farmer and Ph.D. candidate living in Roxbury with his family, met to write a proposal for use of a large parcel of state-owned land in the corridor.

The proposal was written in response to a request for proposals from the city's Comprehensive Employment and Training Act (CETA) program and included plans for a large community garden, solar greenhouse, and educational programs. While the city assessed the proposal's feasibility, the small group incorporated as the Southwest Corridor Community Farm, Inc.

Twenty-one unemployed people eligible for CETA jobs were hired under the terms of the one-year contract, and Jon Ellertson was hired as the farm's director. The group included a broad spectrum of the unemployed: they ranged from young people for whom this was a first job to laid-off union workers nearing retirement age. There were public housing tenants, a Chinese man who had immigrated to the United States via Latin America (he was fluent in both Chinese and Spanish but spoke hardly a word of English), former clerical workers, and several people who had not yet completed their college degrees. The CETA workers represented most of Boston's neighborhoods, most ethnic groups, and reflected most of the city's problems.

Since the project came on the heels of the city's first year of full-fledged school busing, the tensions erupting throughout the neighborhoods tore into the group of CETA workers. One young white woman from Charlestown's Bunker Hill housing project was stoned by neighbors when her picture appeared in a newspaper photograph of the multi-racial group. Relationships among the workers on the site were relatively good, but it was impossible to protect the project and its participants from the often terrifying pressures facing its participants: violence in the streets and sometimes at home, illness of parents and children, and car accidents. One time a car driving by the work site skidded into four cars parked alongside and disappeared, thereby disabling the program's entire fleet. And CETA wages were low.

Without much support from the city's CETA bureaucracy, the project ended 1977 with a miraculous amount of work accomplished: a large community garden had been constructed on the acre site, and it was bordered in back by the first solar-heated community greenhouse in Boston. Some of the program participants went on to jobs in fields related to the program, the most notable success being a laid-off factory worker in his fifties who was so taken by the food preservation workshops that he was later hired by the instructors at the local Extension Service.

The tragedy of the CETA experience was that participants were eligible for only one year. Just as peace, harmony, and efficiency descended on the work site, the program was over and the CETA workers were thrown back on their own resources at a time when jobs and housing were scarce and racial tensions drew sharp lines around neighborhoods, transit corridors, and, therefore, opportunities.

The small group from three neighborhoods who had incorporated to form the Southwest Corridor Farm resigned to enable a more locally based board of directors to be elected. By the end of the summer of 1978 a community of ten people (including several of the former CETA workers) had taken firm control of the greenhouse, the garden plots, and the project's future.

As people joined the farm, claiming plots, planting borders of flowers, and improving the greenhouse, some of the tensions of the underlying community life surfaced: the farm straddled a district of black, white, and Hispanic neighborhoods. Yet the new board consisted primarily of young black and white families, almost all better educated and more instantly committed to the concept of the farm than the predominantly Hispanic residents who lived adjacent to the site. At this juncture the organization needed some way to publicize its commitment to serving the three communities and *all* their residents. Femke Rosenbaum, the Dutch wife of one of the new board members, began to organize a spring celebration to which residents of the three neighborhoods and the site's abutters would be drawn. Rosenbaum worked with a friend and folklorist to research multi-cultural rituals of spring. Weaving together the myths and traditions of ethnic groups represented in the Southwest Corridor (as well as those whose footsteps hardly touched New England soil—like the Norsemen), she inaugurated the annual "Wake Up the Earth Festival" at the farm.

The first festival, in 1978, began with a children's parade which originated in the three neighborhoods and then emerged at the farm. There followed ethnic dances, maypole dances, the sale of seedling vegetables and flowers from the greenhouse, and booths with food and crafts that represented the local communities.

Each year subsequently the Wake Up the Earth Festival has evolved afresh. One year it attracted Japanese Buddhist monks in Boston on an international peace tour; their banners and simple drumbeats dominated the slow, colorful children's parade. The next year an enormous dragon appeared, dancing to a beat known only to itself and its centipedes.

Over the years the Southwest Corridor Farm expanded its scope, its membership, and its impact. Under the direction of first Susan Naimark and then Leroy Stoddard, and with the assistance of Boston Urban Gardeners and local charitable foundations, the farm has rebuilt the original greenhouse, offered educational programs to nearby public elementary schools, and supported five satellite community gardens in the surrounding neighborhoods. The greenhouse has become more and more efficient, producing thousands of seedlings for sale to community gardeners.

As the farm staff and the board's expertise grew, the organization turned to contracted work as a source of additional income. By 1984 the farm crew was clearing brush and mowing entrances to Boston's historic Franklin Park, and had undertaken a contract with the transportation authority to mow newly seeded grass and clover planted along the Southwest Corridor. In 1985 the farm was able to hire one of the graduates of Boston Urban Gardeners' Landscape Construction Training Program.

Uncertainty about long-term tenure of the land, however, always shadowed the farm's progress. Its parcel was owned by the Massachusetts Bay Transportation Authority, which did not show "community gardening" on its maps of projected land use. Located adjacent to the now almost completed and speculatively "hot" Southwest Corridor, and abutting a neighborhood that suffered from a severe housing shortage, its acre was viewed as highly "developable" by both housing advocates and for-profit development interests. Caught between an ideological commitment to housing for its low-income neighbors and the need for productive open space for community use and new private market employers, the farm's staff struggled to be sensitive to other community demands while publicizing its own claims.

In 1985, through a grant from the local Parker Foundation, the Jamaica Plain Community Planning Coalition was formed to provide a forum for the discussion and resolution of these and related issues. The recommendations of its Open Space Committee clearly recognized the importance of open spaces and, if enacted, would protect the farm.

Green space is vital to a liveable city. Greenery provides a balance between the built environment and the natural world. The existence of urban wilds help us appreciate this natural world. Community gardens teach us the value of productive and cooperative work. Neighborhoods where residents are able to gather on the grass are friendlier and healthier. Landscaped sitting areas in commercial districts encourage us to relax, talk to each other, and use our local stores.

In the spring of 1986 the Wake Up the Earth Festival parade traveled the length of the new linear Southwest Corridor parkland, marking the beginning of new life and activity for Corridor communities. Whether the farm will survive on its acre is still uncertain; yet there is every indication that members and supporters have successfully made their case and that the Southwest Corridor Community Farm will emerge from its roots as a one-time-only CETA project to fulfill its promise as a permanent model of active community gardening in the city.

Over the past decade Boston Urban Gardeners (BUG) has grown to be the coordinator of a hundred or so garden associations across the city, associations whose members number five thousand gardeners. These community gardens range in size from a few side-yard plots of four or five gardeners to the large fields of plots in outer Dorchester. BUG's work continues to be both political and technical. It assists gardeners in organizing themselves and in finding lots, it defends existing gardens against plans to sell off the land by calling out the gardeners to protest, it promotes neighborhood farmers' markets, and it carries out educational programs for gardening and home food preservation. On the technical side, it manages a large mulch pile in Hyde Park, seeks soil and water for community gardens, runs a greenhouse to propagate plants and flowers, offers design consulting to community groups, and trains young people in landscaping skills. In the ten years of its existence BUG has become an important social and political institution in the city. The meaning of the community garden movement that BUG embodies and promotes is, however, much larger than an institution, even such a useful and successful one. The meaning of the gardens derives from their role as vehicles for the many traditions which they carry into the city, and from their simultaneous function as propagators of new hopes and new ideas for the design and management of city land.

Visions for a Better Future

The social and political processes of neighborhood organizing for use of vacant land have now been at work in Boston for about a decade. The gardens are the concrete results but by no means the most significant products of people's labor. Out of the experiences of ordinary city dwellers has come a series of goals that propose new directions for the city and its suburbs. The ideas for the future can be arranged in clusters, each grouping organized by the activities that are the main focus of its adherents. The visions range in scale from the intense issues of families, food, and nearby open space, to an intermediate range of neighborhood control of land and housing, to a comprehensive approach to an integrated local and metropolitan design.

The first group keeps the immediate concerns of families, food, raising children, care for the elderly, and neighborhood sociability as its essential targets. Its goals are the empowerment of ordinary citizens who live in the city. Boston Urban Gardeners and its members best characterize this set of goals. For them the community gardens not only provide food but through their politics they help people to organize food cooperatives, farmers' markets, local playgrounds, health facilities, and neighborhood social and educational activities. The garden movement for this group is a program for social reconstruction, a way to increase the power and efficiency of neighborhood self-help activities so that fewer American families will live stranded and helpless within the commercial metropolis.[93]

A second group builds its hopes for the future upon neighborhood redevelopment, especially on the control of land and housing. They see community gardening as an alternative that arose in the face of landlord and municipal neglect, housing abandonment and arson, trash-filled lots, and the threat of resident displacement by public redevelopment and private gentrification. These neighborhood housing groups imagine a future in which land and housing will be controlled by local community development corporations. Such organizations would have a veto power over private development plans, and would be partners in public projects. Their present goals are to see that the elderly are not driven from their apartments and their houses, that low-income families are able to furnish themselves with decent housing, and that redevelopment does not destroy the public spaces of the neighborhoods as private development had done many years before.

The Roxbury Action Program and the Lower Roxbury Development Corporation's success with architect John Sharratt's Mission Park cluster housing are excellent examples of this sort of organization and its activities. The Alianza Hispana and its sister organization, Nuestra Communidad Development Corporation, recently formed in the Dudley Street–Columbia Road–Quincy Street triangle of Roxbury and Dorchester, represent other such groups. In terms of the history of the American metropolis, such undertakings are bringing to the old core city a long-established suburban land-planning technique: the design of new subdivisions as semi-autonomous neighborhood units. This current inner-city movement for local control of land envisions a future metropolis that is more equitable and more habitable because of a politics of neighborhood self-determination and self-reliance.[94] These goals for locally managed redevelopment have found fresh opportunity in the joining together of the job training of Boston Urban Gardeners and Roxbury Community College with Mayor Raymond Flynn's plans for the renovation of the parks of the city. Local contractors are to be favored in this rebuilding and future maintenance; the Afro-American and Hispanic communities will particularly benefit, since most of the city's parks are adjacent to their homes.

The third group sees the community gardens as important elements to be included in designs for improving the natural and human ecologies of the entire metropolis. At present these advocates are landscape professionals, men and women well in advance of conventional urban practices. This group's experience lies with the failures of recent American city building and rebuilding, failures that make it more and more expensive to maintain the metropolis even at lowered and restricted levels of human existence. Good food, air, water, shelter, and recreation have been getting scarcer and scarcer.

For this group the community garden is an integral part of a system of metropolitan planning whose purpose is to design in such a way that the inherited land of the metropolis and the settlement patterns of its inhabitants complement each other. To summarize a complex and sensitive set of proposals, the procedures envision a process whereby community organizations make detailed proposals for land use. These proposals are then reviewed and adjusted in continuing bargaining to establish designs and guidelines that allow the inherited land forms and the human uses to come into mutually sustaining relationships. The goal is not to sacrifice the environment for short-term advantages, and it is not to sacrifice the residents for public and private constructions. Such a program sets norms for the reconstruction of the old core city's abandoned lots, and it also establishes criteria for developing and redeveloping suburbs. The community garden is an important element in such a design, not because it requires much land, but because of what it demonstrates: how people can use land in common for their individual and mutual benefit. This is the essence of all three visions for the future.[95]

Although they focus upon different aspects of today's city, all three of these community garden–related visions rest upon a central truth about cities. All cities are a form of garden. Despite the dominance of streets, highways, and buildings, the city is an assembly of particular environments in which people favor some things and discourage others. What is special about a city is its product, its staple crop. The crop is not plants and animals, but the gardeners themselves.

NOTES TO PART ONE

1. Material concerning the Charlestown garden from an interview with James Hall, June 17, 1986; *Boston Sunday Globe*, July 7, 1985; *Boston Globe*, August 16, 1986, p. 13; and "Endangered Gardens," *The BUG* (spring 1986).

2. Adam Purple's 15,000 square-foot Garden of Eden was at Eldridge Street, between Rivington and Stanton streets; *New York Times*, July 10, 1982, p. 26, and September 4, 1983, p. 49.

3. Robert Orr Whyte, *Rural Nutrition in Monsoon Asia* (London, 1974); Thomas C. Wright, "The Politics of Urban Provisioning in Latin American History," in John C. Super and Thomas C. Wright, *Food, Politics, and Society in Latin America* (Lincoln, Nebr., 1985), 24–45; H. J. Teuteberg, "The General Relationship between Diet and Industrialization," in Elborg and Robert Forster, *European Diet from Pre-Industrial Times* (New York, 1975), 61–67; Vera Ninez, ed., "Household Level Food Production," *Food and Nutrition Bulletin* 7 (September 1985): 1–67; John F. C. Turner, *Housing by People* (New York, 1977).

4. Mark Francis, Lisa Cashdan, and Lynn Paxon, *Community Open Spaces: Greening Neighborhoods through Community Action and Land Conservation* (Covelo, Calif., 1984), 1–27. The book has an excellent bibliography of recent open space literature.

5. Joseph L. Eldredge, *Architecture Boston* (Barre, Mass., 1976), 102–3.

6. Interview with Charlotte Kahn, Boston Urban Gardeners (hereinafter referred to as BUG), June 12, 1986; and information from Paul McCann, general counsel, and Maria Faria, of the Boston Redevelopment Authority, June 30, 1986; *Boston Sunday Globe*, June 29, 1986, p. 27.

7. Tom Fox, Ian Koeppel, and Susan Kellam, *Struggle for Space, The Greening of New York City 1970–1984* (Neighborhood Open Space Coalition, New York, 1985), 21.

8. 1760–1818 enclosures 7,820 sq. miles. England is 50,333 sq. miles; Massachusetts is 7,833 sq. miles. Great Britain, *Departmental Committee of Inquiry into Allotments, Report, October, 1969* (London, H.M.S.O., 1972), 2.

9. *Inquiry into Allotments*, 2.

10. Raymond Williams, *Culture and Society 1780–1950* (London, 1961), 23–39.

11. D. C. Barnett, "Allotments and the Problem of Rural Poverty, 1780–1840," in E. L. Jones and G. E. Mingay, eds., *Land, Labor, and Population in the Industrial Revolution* (New York, 1967), 167.

12. Barnett, 173–74.

13. Barnett, 177.

14. John Stuart Mill, "Of Popular Remedies for Lower Wages," *Principles of Political Economy*, books 1 and 2 (1848), ed. J. M. Robson, *Collected Works of John Stuart Mill* (Toronto, 1956), 355–66.

15. Karl Marx, in describing the impoverishment of the English farm laborer and the prevalent malnourishment of his family, spoke of the importance of small garden plots for such a family's survival. *Capital: A Critique of Political Economy*, vol. 1 (1867), International Publishers, 100th anniversary ed. (New York, 1967), 680–82.

16. *Inquiry into Allotments*, 2–5.

17. The historian of the potato, Redcliffe N. Salaman, in his *History and the Social Influence of the Potato* (Cambridge, England, 1949), 247–48, 525, thought that the allotment gardens of England owed their origins to the examples of the small peasant potato patches of seventeenth-century Ireland.

18. Barnett, 170.

19. Jeanette M. Neeson, "Opposition to Enclosure in Northamptonshire c. 1760–1800," Andrew Charlesworth, "The Rise of an Agricultural Proletariat," and Anne Digby, "Protest in East Anglia against the Imposition of the New Poor Law," all in Andrew Charlesworth, ed., *An Atlas of Rural Protest in Britain 1548–1900* (Philadelphia, 1983), 56–60, 131–39, 158–61. Also *Inquiry into Allotments*, 3.

20. *Inquiry into Allotments*, 14–15.

21. *Inquiry into Allotments*, 10–11.

22. Quoted in Walter Muir Whitehill, *Boston: A Topographical History*, 2d ed. (Cambridge, 1975), 47.

23. Lewis Mumford, *The Culture of Cities* (New York, 1938), 42–51; the gardens of the preindustrial cities can be seen in the atlas of Jan Jensson, *Theatrum Urbium* (Amsterdam, 1657), 8 vols.

24. Stefan Muthesius, *The English Terraced House* (New Haven, 1982), 49–62, 101–42.

25. George Rosen, *History of Public Health* (New York, 1958), 152–76; Mumford, 120–24, 149–68.

26. The guinea was a gold coin issued from 1663 to 1813. It had a value of 21 shillings under the former English monetary system, or 1.05 pounds by current reckoning.

27. *Inquiry into Allotments*, 10.

28. *Inquiry into Allotments*, 11.

29. *Inquiry into Allotments*, map, 9–12, 15.

30. As late as the 1930s the garden clubs of England leased half of their allotment space from private landlords. Lebert H. Weir, *Europe at Play: A Study of Recreation and Leisure Time Activities* (New York, 1937), 260–64.

31. George K. Lewis, "Kleingarten: Evolution of an Urban Retreat," *Landscape* 23, no. 2 (1979): 33–37.

32. Stephan Muzika, "Les jardins ouvriers, du paternalisme social à une appropriation populaire," Ph.D. diss. Université de Paris, Institut d'Urbanisme, November 1984 (copy available at Rotch Library, Massachusetts Institute of Technology), 10–18; Theodore Zeldin, *France 1848–1945: Ambition and Love* (New York, 1979), 265.

33. Lewis, 37; Weir, 264–71. See also C. Lindhagen, "Stockholm Garden Settlements," in League of Nations, *Quarterly Bulletin of the Health Organization* 3 (September 1934): 359–87; for Norway, John Rolfson Haavik, "Kolonihager," *Landscape Architecture* 73 (March–April 1983): 72–73; for Italy, Giulio Crespi, ed., *Orti urbani: una resorsa* (Milan, 1980).

34. Thomas J. Bassett, "Reaping on the Margins: A Century of Community Gardening in America," *Landscape* 25, no. 2 (1981): 1–8; Rufus R. Wilson, "Free Farming for the Poor," *Harper's Weekly* 39 (June 15, 1895): 566; Frederick W. Speirs, Samuel M. Lindsay, and Franklin B. Kirkbride, "Vacant-Lot Cultivation," *Charities Review* 8 (March 1898): 74–78. For a detailed report on the second year in Detroit, see Benjamin O. Flower, "A Successful Experiment for the Maintenance of Self-Respecting Manhood," *Arena* 15 (March 1896): 544–54.

35. Jacob Riis, *How the Other Half Lives* (1890), ed. Sam Bass Warner, Jr. (Cambridge, 1970); Eric E. Lampard, "The Urbanizing World," in *The Victorian City*, vol. 1 (H. J. Dyos and Michael Wolff, eds., London, 1973), 3–57.

36. Industrial Aid Society, *Sixtieth Annual Report* (Boston, 1895), 6–7.

37. *Sixtieth Annual Report*, 7; "Report of the Committee on the Cultivation of Vacant Lots," appended to *Sixtieth Annual Report*, 2.

38. Committee on Vacant Lots, "Report, 1895," 3.

39. Committee on Vacant Lots, "Report, 1895," 4.

40. Industrial Aid Society, *Sixty-second Report* (Boston, 1897), 21–22; Galen Cranz, *The Politics of Park Design* (Cambridge, 1982), 7–15.

41. Industrial Aid Society, *Sixty-third Report* (Boston, 1898), 8.

42. Bureau of Associated Charities of the City of Chicago, *Fourth Annual Report* (Chicago, 1898), 16–17.

43. Chicago Board of Charities, *Cooperation* 1 (January 19, 1901): 4–5.

44. Chicago Bureau of Charities, *Eighth Annual Report* (Chicago, 1902), 13.

45. Chicago Bureau of Charities, *Fifth Annual Report* (Chicago, 1899), 8.

46. *Cooperation* 5 (September 16, 1905): 306; Speirs et al., 82–83.

47. *Cooperation* 5 (June 3, 1905): 173.

48. *Cooperation* 7 (March 23, 1907): 68.

49. L. Margaret Barnett, *British Food Policy during the First World War* (London, 1985), 26, 77; F. E. Green, "The Allotment Movement," *Contemporary Review* 114 (July 1918): 90–96.

50. Charles Lathrop Pack, *The War Gardens Victorious* (Philadelphia, 1919), 12.

51. Charles Lathrop Pack, *Victory Gardens Feed the Hungry* (Washington, 1919), 6–7; Cranz, 251–53.

52. Pack, *War Gardens*, 6; Board of Commissioners, City of Boston Parks and Recreation Department, *43rd Annual Report for the Year Ending January 31, 1918* (Boston, 1919), 3.

53. Pack, *Victory Gardens*.

54. Pack, *Victory Gardens*, 6–7.

55. Pack, *War Gardens*, 16–19, 80.

56. John L. Hancock, "John Nolen and the American City Planning Movement: A History of Cultural Change and Community Response," (Ph.D. thesis, University of Pennsylvania, 1964, University Microfilms, Ann Arbor, Mich.), 368–82; "Mariemont, Ohio," *Architectural Record* 69 (April 1931): 342–45; also, the housing reformer Catherine Bauer cited Plessis-Robinson, a new Paris suburb, as exemplar. It was full of allotment gardens. Bauer, *Modern Housing* (Boston, 1934), plate no. 21.

57. Joanna C. Colcord and Mary Johnston, *Community Programs for Subsistence Gardens* (New York, 1933); Fox, Koeppel, and Kellam, 5–6.

58. "Subsistence Homesteads for Industrial and Rural Workers at the End of 1934," *Monthly Labor Review* 40 (January 1935): 19–37; Paul K. Conklin, *Tomorrow a New World: The New Deal Community Program* (Ithaca, N.Y., 1959).

59. Richard D. Parker, "The Fenway Gardens: A Unique Example of Outstanding Adult Recreation," printed three-page history of the Fenway Garden Society. Papers of the society are deposited in the library of the Massachusetts Horticultural Society, Boston, Mass.

60. BUG "Newsletter," May 1977 (BUG office files); Matthew W. Sheridan, "The Fenway Victory Garden," *Boston Entertaining Arts* (June 1976): 4–6; Commonwealth of Massachusetts, *Journal of the Senate for the Year 1960* (Boston, 1960), 1226; *Boston Globe*, August 4, 1960; conversation with Hon. John E. Powers, May 29, 1985; obituary, Richard D. Parker (1892–1975), *Boston Globe*, August 12, 1975; John McGannon, "An Ageless Tradition Ahead of Its Time," *Brooklyn Botanic Garden Record: Plants and Gardens* 31 (March 1976): 56–57.

61. George Sternlieb, *Tenement Landlord* (New Brunswick, N.J., 1966); Glenn A. Clayton, "Abandoned," *Journal of Housing* 28 (June 1971): 271–76; National Commission on Urban Problems, *Building the American City*, for 91st Congress, 1st Session, *House Document no. 91-34* (Washington, 1968), 102.

62. Robert Fisher, *Let the People Decide: Neighborhood Organizing in America* (Boston, 1984), 110–12; Frances Fox Piven and Richard Cloward, *Regulating the Poor* (New York, 1971).

63. The chronology of a list of important conflicts would order events in the following sequence: 1953, campaigns by Linus Pauling and Barry Commoner, to stop atomic testing on the grounds that it poisons the earth; 1953, U.S.–U.S.S.R. Test Ban Treaty; 1962, on chemical poisoning, Rachel Carson, *Silent Spring;* December 20, 1960, 350 U.S. military advisors in South Vietnam; April 30, 1975, Saigon evacuated; 1959, U.S. food surpluses in the midst of domestic malnutrition and overseas starvation: U.S. Department of Agriculture revives its Depression Food Stamp Program; May 21, 1968, Columbia Broadcasting System documentary "Hunger in America"; 1972, black national-

ism and separatism, Robert Blauner, *Racial Oppression in America*; 1973, decentralization, E. F. Schumacher, *Small Is Beautiful: Economics As If People Mattered* (London, 1973).

64. "Flowers, Gardens Are Found to Provide Big Boost to Public Housing Tenant Morale Coast to Coast," *Journal of Housing* 21 (May 1964): 180–85; Ira S. Robbins, "Tenants' Gardens in Public Housing," in Whitney North Seymour, Jr., ed., *Small Urban Spaces* (New York, 1969), 140.

65. Robbins, 141–45; Charles A. Lewis, "Healing the Urban Environment: A Person/Plant Viewpoint," *American Institute of Planners Journal* 45 (July 1979): 333.

66. Francis, Cashdan, and Paxon, 22–24.

67. Eve Asner, "Philadelphia's Neighborhood Park Program," in Seymour, 176; or "Ghost Buildings Go: Parks Appear," *Journal of Housing* 21 (April 15, 1964): 147–49.

68. Robin C. Moore, "The Diary of a Volunteer Playground," *Landscape Architecture* 63 (April 1973): 216–20.

69. Details of the history of the People's Park may be found in a memorandum of the University of California-Berkeley Public Information Office, "Chronology of Events and Decisions Concerning the Area Known as 'People's Park,'" typescript, November 1979, 14pp.; Alan Copeland, *People's Park* (New York, 1969); and Robert Sommer, *Design Awareness* (San Francisco, 1972). ·

70. Fox, Koeppel, and Kellam, 7.

71. Francis, Cashdan, and Paxson, 29; BUG, "Model Garden Project" (report, 1982, BUG files), 20; Larry Somers, *The Community Garden Book* (Burlington, Vt., 1984), 120–21.

72. *1976 Official Congressional Directory, 94th Congress, 2nd Session* (Washington, D.C., 1976), 124; U.S. Department of Agriculture Extended Food and Nutrition Program, "Guidelines for 1977 EFNEP Urban Gardening Program" (booklet at Suffolk County Agricultural Extension Service, Boston). American Community Garden Association, P.O. Box 93147, Milwaukee, Wisconsin 53202.

73. Boston Redevelopment Authority, Alexander Ganz et al., *The Future of Boston's Poor* (Preliminary Report, Boston, July 1985), table 20.

74. Herbert Gans, *Urban Villagers* (New York, 1962); Langley Carleton Keyes, Jr., *The Rehabilitation Planning Game* (Cambridge, Mass., 1969), 27; Marc Fried, *The World of the Working Class* (Cambridge, Mass., 1973); John H. Mollenkopf, *The Contested City* (Princeton, N.J., 1983), 155–212.

75. Stephan Thernstrom, *Poverty, Planning, and Politics in the New Boston: The Origins of Action for Boston Community Development* (New York, 1969), 7–16, 179–86.

76. *Boston Globe*, April 26–30, 1968; Melvin H. King, *Chain of Change* (Boston, 1981), 111–18; Mel King, "BRA: Guarantee Tent City's Development—Now!" *Boston Business Journal* (August 12–18, 1985), 3B.

77. Richard Hatch, ed., *The Scope of Social Architecture*, New Jersey Institute of Technology, *Columns* 1 (New York, 1984): 202–17.

78. Alan Lupo, Frank Colcord, and Edmund P. Fowler, *Rites of Way: The Politics of Transportation in Boston and the United States City* (Boston, 1971), 22–111.

79. King, *Chain of Change*, 30–46.

80. J. Anthony Lukas, *Common Ground: A Turbulent Decade in the Lives of Three American Families* (New York, 1985).

81. *Boston Globe*, June 2–8, 1967.

82. Alan Lupo, *Liberty's Chosen Home* (Boston, 1977).

83. Boston Redevelopment Authority, *The Future of Boston's Poor*, 7–12, 23–24.

84. For example, Mr. Jesse Bird of 6 Oscar Street began a garden on the vacant lot next to his house in 1968 and has been developing it ever since (interview, July 30, 1984).

85. BUG, "Newsletter," May 1977.

86. Jerry Howard, "The Experiment in Weston," *Horticulture* 54 (May 1979): 22–29.

87. Jeff Sommer, "Luis Lopez and His Garden of Urban Delights," *Boston Phoenix*, September 21, 1976, 45; biography of Melvin H. King, *Boston Globe*, October 5, 1983, 23.

88. Tufts University, Department of Urban and Environmental Policy, *A Land Resource Opportunity: The Reuse of Vacant Lots in Boston* (Medford, Mass., May 24, 1983), 35–37; Jeff Sommer, "Urban Gardening: The Plots Thicken: Cultivating Centers of Caring," *Boston Phoenix*, October 26, 1974, 16–17, 31; Mollenkopf, 128–35.

89. Tufts University, *Land Resource Opportunity*, 1, 19, 38–39.

90. "History of the South End Project," BUG files; Jeff Sommer, "Luis Lopez," *Boston Phoenix*, September 21, 1976, 10, 45.

91. These two case studies have been furnished by Charlotte Kahn, director of BUG, using materials from the organization's files.

92. Alan Lupo, *Boston Globe*, November 30, 1985, p. 19; *Boston Greenspace Alliance Newsletter* 1 (March–April 1986).

93. BUG, ed., Susan Naimark, *A Handbook of Community Gardening* (New York, 1982), 6–15; Judith Joan Wagner, "The Economic Development Potential of Urban Agriculture on the Community Scale," M.S. thesis, M.I.T., 1980, microfiche, Rotch Library, M.I.T.; Michael Hough, "Metro Homestead," *Landscape Architecture* 73 (January–February 1983): 54–58.

94. Steward E. Perry, *Building a Model Black Community: The Roxbury Action Program*, Center for Community Economic Development (Cambridge, Mass., 1978).

95. Anne Whiston Spirn's *The Granite Garden: Urban Nature and Human Design* (New York, 1984) is the leading book today of this school. The fathers of the movement from the professional side are Ian L. McHarg, *Design with Nature* (Philadelphia, 1969), and Kevin Lynch, *A Theory of Good City Form* (Cambridge, 1981). See also Randolph J. Hester, "Process Can Be Style: Participation and Conservation in Landscape Architecture," *Landscape Architecture* 73 (May–June 1983): 49–55.

PART TWO
Portraits

Woman and child
The Community Garden Project, Boston State Hospital, Mattapan

I was born in the country. I love the smell of the dirt, the smell of the grass. So that keeps me going . . . roses, any plant. I love to plant; I love to watch anything grow. I kneel down in that dirt and take up a handful of it. I say this is nature; this is something that cannot be duplicated; this is God's thing and I enjoy it.

—Victor Pomare, Roxbury

People who are interested in housing are interested in housing. That's how you gotta take them. And the people who have gardens are interested in housing and *gardening.*

You can't just say, "Gardens and the hell with housing," or "Housing and the hell with gardening." Everybody's got to get together, and let's figure it out. We've got to keep each other happy.

—*James Hall, Charlestown*

I come from Arkansas, Arkansas to Boston. I was a mile and a half from the Mississippi River. I would get up every morning and look at the levee. When the sun rise, it'll come up over the levee, and I'd be shaded from the sun from the levee every morning.

Farming sure is different now in Arkansas. Gardens down there, everything they done planted been eaten by the middle of June, first of July. . . . Greens, turnips, and like those bunch of beans, they're planting the second crop of them in the middle of the summer, 'cause down there you could plant turnips and cabbage and collards in March or even February. Yeah, you could set them out even in the middle of February.

John Robinson
The Community Garden Project, Boston State Hospital, Mattapan

I have been gardening every year since I started, which was 1942 or '43, without any interruptions. And I didn't want to garden. They had to nearly shove me into it. I just wouldn't do any gardening. I could cook and sew, but deliver me from the garden. Well, one day I was with a friend who had a garden here in the Fens, and this man from the Park Department came up to me and said, "You don't have a garden. And you're going to take that garden (the vacant lot next to my friend's garden) and you're going to dig it up tomorrow." "I don't want a garden," I said. But I came and dug it up the next day just the same, and here I am still gardening some forty years later. And you know it's been a life-saver. I even did it on crutches one time, a couple of times in fact.

Mabel Matheson
The Fenway Victory Garden, The Fenway

I've had gardens, at least my mother and father did, all our lives. When I was a baby they had the garden. This was in Virginia up around the Blue Ridge mountains. We had four acres of our own land. We had a house built on it and everything. And most of my people lived around that section; they mostly Cherokee.

When I first moved in here there were houses all around. So I didn't start to garden until they tore down the first house. The rest of the houses still had people living in them. But when they tore down the first house I started to garden and that's quite a few years ago. Now I wouldn't know just what year it was, but it's been a long time. And every time they tear down a house, somebody else would come in and start a garden. Finally they tore all the old places down.

Jesse Byrd
Oscar Street Community Garden, Jamaica Plain

There are too many senior citizens who sit in the house, look out the window, have nothing to do, but who have a great deal to contribute. And my thing is to get these people out doing something.

I think, over and above getting those people out of the house has been the conviviality that exists when they come out here. They do a little hoeing, they sit down, they chat, they talk about things, and they meet other people. Which gives them, in my opinion, an opportunity to think that, "although I'm 75, I'm somebody. I've got a place to go to garden, and I'll meet some friends out there."

—Edward Cooper, Roxbury

Like I was telling you before, a lot of people will come down here after work and they give their garden maybe half an hour. It's very good mental therapy. It's good for their minds; it's good for their heads. People walk down, they talk. We talk about each other's troubles, and everybody goes home smiling.

—James Hall, Charlestown

Personally I think it is a crime to take these gardens away. I just see too many good things coming out of the gardens. I see people talking to each other even if they can't understand the language. You can communicate in sign language. It's a bridge between minorities and people of different backgrounds. The garden is so positive that to destroy it the city would lose an awful lot.

—Gretta Norton, Bay Village

Thelma and Edward Cooper
Highland Park 400 Survival Garden, Roxbury

I just get a charge out of walking up here, as I did this morning and do three or four mornings a week, and see Mrs. Jones and Mr. Smith picking tomatoes or talking about the weather. And I have in my hand some carrots that I just got from one of my neighbors. And I picked some string beans, and Mrs. Jones said to me, "Mr. Cooper, I haven't had any of your string beans this year!" So I gave her the string beans and she gave me the carrots. Now, this is good for her; it's good for me. And I want to say that I'm bragging when I say that I'll be 82 next September, but being able to get out and come up here and do the many other things that I think I'm doing is good therapy for me! So when I say that I'm doing this for the community, I'm doing this for me too.

Benny Wilson, Magnolia Hall, Elizabeth Burnett
Highland Park 400 Survival Garden, Roxbury

Visitor, Wilhelmina Williams, Annie Gayle
Highland Park 400 Survival Garden, Roxbury

Benjamin and Earlene Scott
Highland Park 400 Survival Garden, Roxbury

Rose Braud and Mattie Davenport
Highland Park 400 Survival Garden, Roxbury

Richard Heath, Israel Cook, Kim Archung
Highland Park 400 Survival Garden, Roxbury

Shanti Ananda, Satyeana and John Ananda, Ishael, Aurovina and Tipareth Ananda
Highland Park 400 Survival Garden, Roxbury

I don't care how bad your night's been, how bad the morning looks, when you look out and there's a flower, there's life; there's a bird sitting in the tree in the feeder, in the birdbath, it can give you a mood you didn't have when you got up. There's nothing more beautiful in this world than nature, as far as I'm concerned. And we have it, thank God, right here in our own garden.

—Evelyn McMahon, Brighton

And you do get close to people in a garden. For example, Adam Washington, one of the gardeners, died a few months ago. He died on Christmas day. And it was one of the times that I realized, you know, a real sense of linking with families! Because I don't know about Adam; I don't know anything about Adam's history. I just know he was an awfully nice guy, who had a real open heart. He was a key person in the garden, a loving, giving person and I just felt devastated when he died. It's a real loss for the garden and it really made me see that you get awfully close to people, in a way you don't realize, when you're talking over tomatoes.

—Alice Nelson, Dorchester

Tuey Har Lee
Torre Unidad Community Garden, South End

Maria Ortiz and Joseph Howko
Rutledge and Washington Streets Community Garden, South End

Catherine Noseworthy and Carol Cleary
Faneuil Public Housing Development, Brighton

Eloise Pate and children
Harrison and Plympton Streets Community Garden, South End

John Berlandi
Old Colony Public Housing Development, South Boston

Margaret Egan
Old Colony Public Housing Development, South Boston

That lot was on a fringe neighborhood—nobody watching it. And trucks would come and dump junk on it, so it meant there were rats and filth. So one day Sis and I were drinking tea and just talking and we said, "let's clean it up; let's do it!" And we went out there one Saturday with shovels and rakes; and Matt came along, and Sis and Sis's daughters and their husbands, and their children, and then the children up the street. And then the other kids in the street see you working up there and they wonder: what's going on?

The thing about a neighborhood such as ours is people are up for action. You know, when the ambulance comes by everybody turns out of their house and the same thing when you see a group of people around. Everybody, it brings everybody out of their houses and everybody wonders: what's going on? And people may not be doing anything so they'll come and join along. And that's really helpful. . . .

. . . And so on Saturday morning we got a lot of cleaning done. We ended up just raking and raking, and even little kids like Hubie, who was only four years old at the time, would be out with their rakes. They just wanted to be like the adults and older kids, raking and cleaning up. And, boy, we spent all spring doing that and whenever we had free time, we'd go out there and more kids would come. And then we decided if we don't do anything it's just going to get dumped on again. So we thought, "Well, let's put some gardens in here." Actually, that was the idea of the children. They had that idea. They said, "Well, let's put gardens in here." . . .

Dionne, Rocky, Earlena, Tamicka, Rina, Nina
Green Village Garden, Dorchester

. . . And it became like a play area or a get-together area for the kids as well. And you'd look out your window in the morning, and while kids were waiting to go to school, they'd be running around the garden plots, or looking in. And the children would go out into the garden at times that you were surprised. They really kept an eye on their garden.

—Alice Nelson, Dorchester

Tamicka, Rina, Nina
Green Village Garden, Dorchester

I mean, what's the difference between a child living in the city and enjoying a butterfly flying around or a caterpillar or whatever and a child in the country? We're entitled to those things too. Our children should see those things too and enjoy them.

—*Marcia Chaffee, South End*

. . . One little girl, who planted cucumbers the first year, had so many cucumbers she couldn't eat them all, was giving them away to everyone. This was one of the tiny box gardens that's smaller than this table. The second year she planted them again because she had so much fun the first time. Every year she's planting cucumbers and she's getting more all the time! I don't know if it's the dirt in her bed or not, but she is amazing! They are like the weeds in her garden, the cucumbers! And that's fun, because there's just a real pride. You see the pride in the eyes of the kids when something's really coming up. They bring their friends over, and they say, "This is my garden."

—Alice Nelson, Dorchester

Earlena
Green Village Garden, Dorchester

Orchard Park Public Housing Development, Roxbury

You look at this place. It's overgrown, but it really fills an important need. We've got plenty of trees. A blue jay or cardinal flies by, and right around the corner's a busy street with buses and trucks . . . this is a little island in all this madness.

—Rick De Angelis, Dorchester

There were lots of old mattresses and beer cans and things on it, and little trees, wild trees on it. I went to the city and asked them if I could clear it up, because I had a house right in front of it. I bought that house in front of it. And I wanted it to be clean. I want anywhere I am to be clean and have flowers or trees or roses or something. They told me I could go ahead with it, but they didn't have any money to give me to help clean it. I told them, "it's quite all right. I just want to know that I can keep it clean."

—Victor Pomare, Roxbury

They say, "Oh, it's been vacant for twenty-five years." But it's ten years that we've had it. It was vacant for fifteen years, but for ten years we've taken good care of it; we did something with it; we produced something. We put these trees in. See that crimson maple, that was the first tree we planted. We put those arbors in. We've got apricot, peach, three types of apples, a massive rhubarb patch, three hundred raspberry bushes, and so much more. You cannot move this. We could never catch up and make up for what we put in here. We made something out of nothing.

—James Hall, Charlestown

East Brookline and Saint George Streets Community Garden, South End

Rutland and Washington Streets Community Garden, South End

James Hall
Sullivan Square Community Garden, Charlestown

I was born here in Charlestown, 1930. I'm 56 years old just a few weeks ago. But all through my life, we've gardened. My father used to send us out before school in the morning. We'd take the basket with the string on it, and pick up the horse manure. We used to call them road apples. And a lot of people knew then what road apples are. And we used to put them underneath the rose bushes.

Now first thing I do when I get out of work, I go home and change into my work clothes, my farm clothes, call them what you want, but this is where I come every day, to the garden. Like I said, I was an alcoholic one time. It was eight, ten years ago that I made my first move to stop drinking. I found out that there are a lot of nice things to do in this world besides drinking or hanging around a barroom. It's such a waste in a person's life. You know, I just can't believe that I'm involved here, in this beautiful garden, and that I helped to create all this. It took time; it took a lot of hours. My father, God's mercy on him, he always said, "There's never enough light in the day, boy, to do what you want to do." And it's so true.

Joseph Ciampa
Marginal Street Community Garden, East Boston

I come from the old country, from Italy. We had a garden there. Some people, they don't like to farm; it's a lot of work. I know it's a lot of work, but I enjoy myself. And some people don't know how they got to do it, plant a garden. Like the younger generation. They never see it done. But, I mean, when you got it in the blood yourself, you know how to do it and you really like to see things grow.

Collin Simmons
Bromley Heath Housing Development, Jamaica Plain

My grandmother, she always had a garden, that was back in North Carolina, where I was born. And I always worked with her in the garden. So when I came up here, I just found a spot and I've been doing gardening ever since.

. . . And I meet a lot of people through the garden—but then to me there ain't no strangers. Everyone I meet I'm friendly with and then they friendly back. My grandmother always said, "Treat others as you want to be treated yourself," and that's my way. It's like the good book say; it's in the Bible: as you sow so shall you reap.

Gong and Shui Lum
Torre Unidad Community Garden, South End

Kim Suey Lee
Torre Unidad Community Garden, South End

Lee Shee Chin
Torre Unidad Community Garden, South End

PART THREE

The Histories
Within the Gardens

FOR THE COMMUNITY GARDENERS

themselves, their gardens have many meanings: the pleasures and defeats of a season's gardening, the delight and value of the foods grown, and the year-round sociability and politics of the community garden of which their plot is a part. Yet, for the modern city as a whole these community gardens carry many meanings. They gather into the city traditions drawn from all over the world, thereby helping to sustain an invaluable quality of metropolitan life: the generative nature of cultural variety.

Gardens as Cultural Histories

Gardening traditions, like those of sports, crafts, art, music, literature, and religion, stand as intermediaries between the merely personal and the powerful blare of the dominant commercial and official cultures. They help us to find a shared path with like-minded citizens instead of condemning us to a lone journey amidst the clamorous crowds of uniformity. Gardens accomplish this service through the modest and commonplace expressions of ordinary people, without the necessity for large institutions, heavy subsidies, elaborate public relations campaigns, or expensive programs.

The force of cultural variety is exerted only within the domination of the host city itself. All cities function both as disciplinarians and as givers of new opportunities, and food preferences and food habits are not exempt from this treatment. After all, people come to the city seeking work, and here is offered a range of occupations from streetsweeper to radiologist that cannot be found in the countryside. Yet a pressure for conformity accompanies this list of opportunities. The city's rhythms are not to be denied. You must work when others work, and therefore you must eat when others eat. Also, because most newcomers to the city start with low wages they must buy what is easiest to come by and what is cheap. So, for example, the big breakfast of the rural South, meat, eggs, and cornbread, must be replaced with breakfast cereals and squishy white bread; hot dogs and hamburger become staple meats.[1]

Although newcomers must follow the city's time clocks and adjust to its markets, they need not abandon the pleasures of their customs during leisure times. The community garden is thus an adjunct to the "down home" Sunday dinner, the party with the family and fellow countrymen, or the national festival or religious feast day. It is also an opportunity for those with country skills to exercise them and to feel the pleasure of mastery over the natural world which surrounds them.[2] A study of Kansas City showed that everyone in that city, newcomer and old resident alike, shared a core diet, but for treats, for special occasions, and for sport and pleasure, everyone also maintained his distinct tradition: some by gardening, some by fishing, some by hunting, and some by all three.[3] The recent inflation in food prices has added a cash incentive to these leisure practices.

Now urban gardeners can save several hundred dollars by working their community plots.[4]

Gardening, even gardening in public on a community garden, is a liberal activity. You do not have to give up your culture to be a city gardener. There is no one right way to grow vegetables and flowers, because within the broad limits of urban climates all the world's agricultural traditions will succeed. Whatever the local climate affords you may grow. Indeed, the concrete, bricks, asphalt, furnaces, and air conditioners of the city have a warming effect on local climates and thereby stretch out the vegetable season by a few weeks.

All newcomers start out by planting what they know from their own past. For example, southern gardeners try sweet potatoes and okra in Boston; the Chinese plant their hairy squash and bitter melons; the Puerto Ricans tend their cilantro, which is the same plant (*Coriandrum sativum*) as the Chinese *yuen tsai* and the Bible's coriander.[5] Mediterranean Bostonians from Italy, Greece, and Lebanon carefully tend their tender grape vines (*Vitis vinifera*) which are a different species from the native Concord grape (*Vitis labrusca*). If you walk about Boston today examining the different community gardens closely, you will find, in one or another plot, almost all the food plants of the world, and most of the gardening techniques of the various peoples and various regions of the earth. Only, the cold winters of most North American cities forbid some tropical plants and tropical farming practices.

This gift to the city's culture is part of an ongoing historical process in which people, plants, and methods of cultivation are in continual change. City dwellers learn from each other and quickly adopt each other's ways: the Italian fondness for basil has recently become a general American fashion; corn appears in Chinese dishes; and the Chinese system of raised bed horticulture attracts American gardeners.[6] Thus, each garden plot is both a continuation of a long history and a part of today's ongoing cultural processes.

Within the gardens themselves history advances at several very different paces. One pace, the slowest, is the process of the domestication of wild plants. This is the slow sequence by which human beings adapted to plants and plants adapted to humans. The world vegetable list emerged from these thousands upon thousands of years. A second pace is the process of formation of the world's regional diets, cuisines, and agricultures. For convenience this pace can be imagined as having a speed of recorded human history, say a pace of five thousand years. A third pace is the swiftly moving sequence of events of the modern world itself: the explosion of changes that set in after Columbus's discovery of the New World. This recent history is the story of the migrations of millions of people from continent to continent, the opening up of vast new agricultural regions, and the urbanization of mankind. These three different sequences of change, each one with its unique cultural meanings, are brought together in even the smallest garden plot.

Consider, for a moment, the few rows of sweet corn that stand up in some city gardens during the late summer. The corn (*Zea mays*) is being grown as a delicacy. It is the sweet corn that flourishes in country and suburban gardens and is one of the delights of the American cuisine. In keeping with the fastest pace of change, the city dweller is growing corn because he is a part of a cultural chain of learning and teaching which stretches back to the late eighteenth century when the Indians of New York, the Six Nations, taught the English settlers how to eat corn as a green vegetable.

The Indian use of the plant invokes a slower-moving clock: theirs was the pace of the formation of diet, cuisine, and agricultural practices. The Indians of the two Americas developed one of the world's basic diets—the corn, bean, and squash diet. Archaeological remains show that this diet has been in place at least since 2,500 B.C. The corn of the Indians, however, was not one variety but many different kinds, each favored because of its different use.

In the long spine of mountains that stretches from the Andes through Mexico, Indians tended many varieties of sweet corn, corns with short cobs, round ends, irregular rows of kernels, and kernel colors that ranged from white to deep red. They used these sweet corns for roasting and boiling, for dried meal, for pounding into a powder to make sugar, for fermenting into an alcoholic drink, and for religious ceremonies. This wide range of human uses meant that the Indians encouraged the variation that naturally occurs in any species, and that they favored varieties and hybrids that were sugary. Such use and selection constitutes a very important stage in a plant's history. Human beings by encouraging the variations in a species thereby make it possible for the plant to flourish in many different settings, and they thereby prepare it for later migrations around the globe. Because of such a long historical process none of the cultivated vegetables today is fussy; they all can be grown in many different environments.

In this region of many varieties of corn, some sweet corn hybridized with some starchy corns (corns like today's field, or cattle, corns) to produce a long-eared, regular-row, yellow-kernel corn much like grandfather's prized Golden Bantam. This variety then migrated east from the Great Plains of North America to the Northeast. It was favored by the Indians of the Northeast because they did not use corn for sugar but only boiled, roasted, and dried it. This was the variety of corn, and the cluster of uses, which the Indians taught the Europeans. Yet the earlier and more various corns of Mexico and Central America still exist, and they provide the genetic pool out of which today's plant breeders dip for the "inventions" of next winter's seed catalogue.[7]

Finally, behind the stages of the years of history and archaeology lies the long and unknown period of domestication itself. It seems likely that the first domestication of corn took place somewhere in the Andes. There men and women took the earliest steps toward the domestication of the wild ancestors of today's city garden corn. Perhaps they merely picked the grass, or used its ears for some religious purposes. Because it was being picked the corn began to travel about, meet new circumstances; variations were encouraged. The early corn users must have favored some varieties over others, and in time they took up cultivating the plant.

This process of human and plant interaction went on for many centuries, indeed for so many centuries that the wild ancestors of modern vegetables have died out. Yet, startling though it seems in the face of modern plant science and food experimentation, no plant eaten by modern man was not eaten or used by prehistoric man! In prehistory all our vegetable species came into being. Humans have stopped eating many plants, but we have added no new species to our tables except the strawberry, an eighteenth-century hybrid. Today's big city vegetable garden is thus the carrier of a line of human experience which stretches continuously back to our hunting and gathering ancestors.[8]

Thanks to the planting of community gardens on the vacant lots of the city, one of the urban pleasures of the United States is community-garden watching. A walk about most neighborhoods will turn up a great variety of vegetables, many distinct methods of cultivation, and gardeners who carry plant and gardening traditions from all across the nation and from all over the world. The history of the plants they grow is not readily available, but the cumulation of works in archaeology, botany, biology, anthropology, history, and geography makes it possible to assemble a brief sketch of most vegetables. The long processes of domestication, of course, cannot be known, but they can be summarized in the form of an estimate of the region of origin for a given plant. The second stage, the five thousand years of archaeological and historical time, is full of gaps, but some major events are recorded. Finally, the modern pace of world migrations of people and plants is well documented. In the case of the United States, the plants came pretty much on the timetables of the immigrants. So the English brought the cabbage, the Africans the melons, and the string beans and pumpkins were here with the Indians to welcome them both.

To enhance the pleasure of urban community gardeners, and to encourage the informed garden watcher, we have listed the plants commonly grown in Boston's garden plots and arranged them according to the migrations of peoples: the Anglo-Irish garden and the Afro-American garden, which represent the early migrations from the seventeenth to the mid-nineteenth centuries; the Italian garden and the Chinese garden, which represent late nineteenth- and early twentieth-century migrations; and the Hispanic garden, which dates from the post–World War II immigration of Puerto Ricans to Boston. Other cities offer different histories and different vegetable lists: German, Norwegian, Japanese, Mexican, Vietnamese and so forth. But even the five Boston examples embrace the world from the Andes to the Himalayas, from Siberia to the African equator.[9]

The Anglo-Irish Garden

Bostonians with backyards have been growing vegetables since the first settlement of the city in 1630. Many of the descendants of the British and Irish migrations, however, have been crowded into apartments or houses whose yards serve only as parking places for automobiles. In recent years some of these citizens have joined their neighbors in establishing community gardens, and on such occasions they have often planted the traditional vegetables of the standard American cuisine: peas, radishes, lettuce, beets, carrots, green beans, cucumbers, squash, onions, tomatoes, and cabbage.

Peas (*Pisum sativum*) are the first seeds planted in a Boston garden. A local saying calls for planting them on St. Patrick's Day, 17 March, even though the ground is cold and often blanketed with a fresh snowfall. The pea is an extremely ancient vegetable; indeed it is known only as a cultivated plant and has no wild forms. The plant is thought to have had its origins in the Mediterranean and also in Afghanistan. Ancient small, round, smooth peas, seeds much like some of our modern varieties but smaller, have been excavated from Swiss lake dwellings of 3000 B.C., and others were dug from the site of the ancient city of Troy. Peas were not found in Egyptian tombs, however, and they migrated only slowly to China, reaching there during the seventh century A.D.

In Europe peas were grown for storing as dried seeds, and the "pease porridge" of the nursery rhyme was a dish made from dried peas, much like pea soup or lentil soup today. During the seventeenth century the Dutch taught the English and the French to cook peas as a fresh vegetable, and there followed a wave of fashion for eating green peas. By a similar quirk of fashion, one of the earliest English varieties of peas was a sugar pea with an edible pod (*P. sativum macrocarpon*), which long passed out of favor but is now enjoying a vogue as a pleasant imitation of the Chinese taste for cooked pea pods.

Very often radishes (*Raphanus sativus*) are planted at the same time as the peas in Boston gardens. Indeed, the radish is the plant Americans use to teach their children about gardening because it comes up so quickly and can so soon be eaten. Radishes, however, are not a toy vegetable but very important members of Mediterranean, Near Eastern, and Oriental cuisines.

The domesticated radish has a wild relative (*R. raphanistrum*), which flourishes as a weed in all the world's Mediterranean climates, including California. It seems likely that the plant domesticated itself by finding a comfortable spot as a weed among the settlements of mankind. Whatever the long domestication process, at the dawn of history the Egyptians were eating radishes in quantity. The Greek historian Herodotus (c. 484–420 B.C.) mentions them as a food of pyramid builders (*History*, 2:125). The British did not make much use of radishes in their diet, but the plant was an important ingredient in

Anglo-Saxon medicine, being prescribed for headaches, shingles, pain, depression, and madness.

Lettuces (*Lactuca sativa*) are very ancient vegetables whose origin is unknown. The milky stems and the leaves have both long been prescribed as medicines. The Greeks and the Romans used lettuce to settle the stomach and to induce sleep at the end of dinner. On other occasions they offered lettuce with radishes at the start of the meal to arouse guests' appetites. The Egyptians grew some form of lettuce, and the biblical Jews ate a lettuce as one of the bitter herbs to accompany the Pascal lamb (Exodus 12:9). This herb, however, may have been chicory, a lettuce relative that grows wild all over Europe, Mediterranean Africa, and the Near East.

There are three basic types of lettuce, the crispy-leaved, the round-headed, and the cylindrical-headed. The last is known as the romaine, or Cos, variety. It gets its name through a corruption of the word "Roman," and Cos is a variation of the spelling of the Greek island of Kos. This type came late to Britain and to New England, being introduced to England only in the reign of Charles I (1625–49). Lettuces, however, were brought to the Americas by Columbus on his second voyage of 1493–96. They spread rapidly through the early settlements so that a century later lettuce was being eaten for salads in Brazil, Mexico, and Quebec.[10]

It seems most likely that beets (*Beta vulgaris*) were first taken up by man for their green leaves and only later cultivated for their roots. The practice of extracting sugar from beets was an eighteenth-century invention. The modern vegetable probably descended from a highly variable species of wild beet (*B. maritima*) which grows on the seacoasts of Europe and Asia. Such plants are called sea-kale beets in Ireland, and their leaves are fed as a cure to sickly sheep. Another possible parent of the garden beet is the wild *Beta petula* of Portugal and the Canary Islands. These European beets have long yellow roots, and yellow beets are still grown in Europe. The red beet is an Italian variety which was perfected in France during the early nineteenth century.

Wild carrots (*Daucus carota*) thrive in the sandy vacant lots of American cities and flourish in the old fields and abandoned farm lands of North America. The tall plant sports an umbrella of white flowers which lends the plant its common name: Queen Anne's lace. It apparently came to the New World with the first settlers from Europe.[11] Just how the cultivated varieties of carrot (also *D. carota*) are related to the ubiquitous wild flower has yet to be determined.

The greatest diversity of carrots occurs in Afghanistan, and so this region is thought to be the vegetable's most likely place of origin. The Greeks and the Romans did not make much of carrots in their cuisine, probably because in the heat of the Mediterranean climate the plants form bitter roots. Carrots were, however, imported from Gaul

(France), and the Arabs grew them in Spain. The Chinese seem also to have been slow to incorporate the carrot into their diet, the earliest mention of the vegetable there being the thirteenth century A.D. The Dutch are the developers of the modern garden varieties. They made a specialty of carrots and introduced their selections into England.

The green bush and pole beans of Boston gardens (*Phaseolus vulgaris*) are descendants of plants that were widely cultivated by prehistoric Indians. Like many vegetables long associated with human beings, the common bean has an extraordinary variability, with over five hundred varieties bearing separate names. The pea bean and navy bean, the beans of Boston's famous baked beans, are two such.

The American Indian's beans were not the beans of the English or Europeans. Europeans grew quite a different plant, the broad bean, or fava (*Vicia faba*), which was an ancient plant of North Africa or Persia. The English called the American vegetable "French beans" because of their route to England: Samuel de Champlain (1567–1635) had brought seeds of American beans to France from his Canadian and New England explorations. They soon proved popular in France; hence the British thought of them as a French invention.

The cucumber (*Cucumis sativas*) is another biblical plant, having been fed by the pharaohs of Egypt to the slaves who built the pyramids. "Think of the fish we used to eat free in Egypt, the cucumbers, melons, leeks, onions, and garlic!" the Jews cried during their flight from Egypt when they tired of eating manna (Numbers, 11:5–6). Cucumbers slaked the workers' thirst and filled them up. The vegetable was immensely popular with all classes from princes to slaves. India seems to have been the original home of the cucumber; from there it traveled west to pharaonic Egypt and east to China, mention being made of the vine in China during the second century A.D.

Columbus planted cucumber seeds, and by 1494 the vines were growing nicely on an island in the Caribbean, Santo Domingo (Columbus's "Hispaniola"). Indians spread the seed throughout the New World, so that when Hernando de Soto invaded Florida in 1539 he was surprised to find the plants already growing prolifically there. In 1535, far to the north, Jacques Cartier recognized cucumbers when he visited Indian villages along the St. Lawrence River.[12]

When they plant their summer squashes (*Cucurbita pepo*), Boston gardeners continue the ancient Indian diet of squash, beans, and corn. Indeed, "squash" is an Algonquin word which has entered the English language. The Indians' name was *askoot asquash* meaning "something eaten green." Seeds of squashes have been unearthed in Mexico which date as far back as 5500 B.C. Like all such long associates of man, these vegetables appear in a tremendous range of varieties. The old warty garden crookneck squash (*C. moschata*) is the close relative of the pumpkin (*C. pepo*), while the small, smooth yellow summer squash and the prolific Italian zucchini are both variations on the pumpkin itself. All these squashes are American plants, although authorities are still in doubt about the starting place of the great Hubbard and turban squashes (*C. maxima*).

The onion (*Allium cepa*) is another of the biblical plants. A member of the lily family, it was often pictured in Egyptian tomb paintings. In their homesickness for the foods of Egypt (Numbers 11:5) the Jews recalled the major forms of the vegetable: "leeks [*A. porrum*], onions [*A. cepa*], and garlic [*A. sativum*]." The plant itself is thought to have had its origins in Central Asia and thence to have spread by migrations across the globe, where in different regions users have encouraged its variations as chives, shallots, green bunching onions, and most recently the tiny cocktail onion.

Tomatoes, perhaps today the quintessential vegetable garden plant (*Lycopersicon esculentum*), were natives of the Andes, where they still grow wild. Mexico has been established as the likely site of domestication. There one Indian language (Nahuatl) names the plant *tomatl*, and well before the Conquest tomatoes had become basic ingredients in the Mexican diet. After the capture of Mexico City in 1519, the seeds traveled east to Europe, where for centuries the plant remained a minor garden curiosity and medicine, except in Italy. The tomato is a relative of the nightshade family (*Solanaceae*), whose members include the poisonous belladonna and the mandrake. Like them, the tomato contains a mildly toxic alkaloid in its leaves and in its green fruit, but it breaks down as the fruit ripens and turns red.

Thomas Jefferson planted tomatoes and made notes about various ways of cooking them. In 1820 one Robert Gibbon Johnson created a small scandal by publicly eating a tomato on the courthouse steps at Salem, New Jersey; yet despite Johnson's bold demonstration the plant's poisonous reputation persisted even into the twentieth century. In the late nineteenth century canned tomatoes, chili sauce, and ketchup began to capture American tastes, but the tomato did not become a major vegetable here until the 1920s. It is not a fruit with many nutritional gifts, but now Americans eat it in such quantities that the tomato has become a major element in our diet. Its color, its flavor—at least in its homegrown state—and its versatility in cooking account for its recent triumph.[13]

The last harvest of the fall is the cabbage (*Brassica oleracea*), a plant of the seacoasts of Europe that was probably first cultivated for its seeds in order to make them into oil. In India today the local species of *Brassicas*, mustards, are grown for their oil seeds and for cattle fodder, and it is the offspring of such plants that flourish across the world as the persistent mustard weeds of farm fields and gardens. Because there are a number of cabbages, turnips, and mustards that grow wild in Europe, they provided the genetic stock for the many modern varieties of cabbage vegetables. The tightly headed common cabbage (*B. oleracea*) was known in Roman times, and its head size has been enlarged since then by selection.

Among other garden cabbages broccoli (*B. oleracea italica*) was an invention of the Italians, and kohlrabi (*B. oleracea gonglyodes*) came out of Hungary and Austria during the sixteenth century. Turnips (*B. rapa*) were the filling vegetable of northern Europe until the American white potato displaced them during the nineteenth century. The American name for turnip, rutabaga, recalls this northern history: the Swedish name for turnip is *rotabagge*. The Brussels sprout (*B. oleracea gemmifera*) has its obscure origins in the Middle Ages. No one knows how the English came to give the plant its Belgian name. The cauliflower (*B. oleracea botrytis cauliflora*) may have been known to the Romans, but it definitely was cultivated by the Arabs in Spain during the twelfth century. Italian merchants imported it from Lebanon and Syria during the sixteenth century. Then the Dutch took it up, and in Queen Elizabeth's time (1558–1603) it was a culinary fad in England. The first American importers, however, were the Spanish, who introduced it to Haiti, where it was reported flourishing already by 1565.

In sum, what makes the Boston Anglo-Irish garden a typical American garden is its diversity. Its vegetables carry the history of many regions and cultures; their ancestors came from Asia Minor, the Mediterranean, and Latin America. All species had achieved their modern varietal forms by the time of Columbus's discovery of the New World. With the exception of the tomato, all the vegetables appeared early in the first European settlers' gardens. Peas, radishes, lettuce, beets, carrots, green beans, cucumbers, squash, onions, and cabbage were grown in the Pilgrim gardens of Plymouth Colony.[14]

Today Boston urban gardeners employ methods of cultivation that reveal northern patterns of land use and northern climatic expectations. Plants are grown in orderly rows on a level garden with the weeds chopped down in the paths and the vegetables watered from a hose or sprinkler, not irrigated by channels of water. Only the vines, the tomatoes and the beans, are tied up; the rest make their way "on the flat." As a gardening technique these methods resemble the improved northern European and New England farm practices of the late eighteenth and early nineteenth centuries, modified only by the substitution of row cultivation for the more frequent use of hills, which was common a hundred years ago.

The Afro-American Garden

Boston's Afro-American gardens gather up three different traditions. They are first of all Boston gardens. Accordingly, they are as full of lettuce, tomatoes, green beans, onions, and summer squash as any in the city. Second, they are gardens whose plantings recall the southern origins of the gardeners' families. The selection of plants reflects the major elements of the diet of the American South. It was the Afro-Americans, after all, who were the cooks in the Confederacy, and it was they who brought African plants and African ways of cooking to the region.[15] The third element is the continuation of the seventeenth-century southern selection of Indian and English plants: the three staples, corn, beans, and squash, were the center of the Indian diet, while the collards came from England.

The sweet potato (*Ipomoea batatas*) is often planted in Boston gardens. We call it by the mistaken name of "yam" because our American usage descends from Africa. Both the tuber we call sweet potato and the tuber we call yam are genetically defined as sweet potatoes. It is, in fact, a South American plant. This potato had been domesticated by Indians as early as 2500 B.C. and had been carried by Polynesians to New Zealand before the Conquest. The Spanish and Portuguese spread the plant across Asia and Africa. One of the true yams, a yellow one (*Dioscorea cayenensis*), was, and still is, a native staple of West Africa. It lent its Senegalese name to the American sweet potato, "yam."[16]

Boston gardeners who raise peanuts (*Arachis hypogaea*) often follow the southern style of preparation: they boil the nuts instead of roasting them. Despite its presence in a northern city, and its ubiquity in the South, the worldwide spread of the peanut is startling.

It was long believed that the peanut was an African or Asian native, introduced into the New World by Portuguese settlers in Brazil. For example, a botanist reviewing the evidence of the abundance of peanuts in Indo-China and equatorial Africa reasoned that the plant originated in south China and then traveled westward. Its popularity in Asia and Africa fooled him.

All the known species of the genus *Arachis* are natives of tropical America. Peanuts have been found as decorative motifs on ancient Peruvian pottery, and the nuts have been dug from prehistoric graves. There is no question that somehow the plant traveled in pre-Columbian times either to China or to Africa, or both. Interestingly enough, the Harvard botanist Oakes Ames, when seeking to establish this history, analyzed peanuts he found in 1917 in Boston's Chinatown and found them to be the same as American peanuts.[17]

A popular South American plant which often appears in Afro-American gardens is the lima bean (*Phaseolus lunatus*). Archaeologists digging in Peru have discovered lima beans that date back to 5000 and 7000 B.C. The Spanish shipped these beans to the Philippines and slave traders brought them to Africa. Limas are now a very important food crop in both Burma and tropical Africa.

Curiously enough, the sixty-odd species that make up the bean genus *Phaseolus* have two distinct continental origins: South America or China, and India. Beans from each area were domesticated and developed entirely separate from one another. The American bean group, the kidney, string, lima, and pea beans, are comparatively large, grow in flattened pods, and often have seeds of many colors and markings. By contrast, the Oriental beans, like the mung bean (*P. aureus*), known to us all as the bean-sprout bean, grow in slender round pods, and are small and comparatively uniform in color.

Best known and most popular of all the African plants that appear in American gardens are the melons (*Cucumis melo*). The African muskmelons, cantaloupes, and casabas are universally popular. Mention of a "melon patch" even appears in the Bible (Isaiah 1:8). Most of the melons are African plants, but there are a number of species from India and a great range of variation among the Indian melons. In the Orient the elongated types of melons are grown as vegetables, and today, both in Africa and in the Orient, they are cooked, rather than eaten raw for dessert like the melons of American gardens.

The watermelon (*Citrullus vulgaris*) has produced a head-on conflict among botanical authorities. Both sides agree that the wild plant that grows in the savannas of Africa is small, bitter, and not good eating. From linguistic evidence Andrew Watson reasons that, like the cucumber, the sweet watermelon was the product of African and Indian exchange. He argues that the melon was domesticated in India and then carried by the Muslims back to Africa, where it has since thrived. He quotes a thirteenth-century author who wrote that the watermelons of the city of Aswan on the Nile River were growing so large that it required a stout camel to transport two of them. Oakes Ames, on the other hand, says that the pharaonic Egyptians were cultivating modern watermelons. For evidence he cites the presence of a melon leaf found in a mummy case. Watson did not refer to the discovery of this leaf, or perhaps he thought it was not the leaf of a sweet watermelon.[18]

However it came to be, the watermelon flourished, and still flourishes, in Africa, and it was carried to America with the slave trade.

Another African migrant in American vegetable gardens is okra (*Hibiscus esculentus*). In warm climates like the southern states, it grows to be a tall plant, four to six feet high. Its pods can be eaten raw or cooked. In the American South, and in Mediterranean cookery, okra is used to thicken soups and stews. The name "okra" descended from the Ghana Tshi language. The other common name, "gumbo," began in Angola as "ki-ngomo," then became the Portuguese word "quin-gumbo," and finally in the West Indies was shortened to just "gumbo."

The collards, or greens, of the Afro-American garden are European plants (*Brassica oleracea*). The very name collard is a corruption of an old English word for cabbage, "colewort." The collards are non-heading cabbages which were brought by the English colonists to Virginia, where they became the major southern green because, unlike the head cabbage, they stand the heat well. Another name for collards is the Scottish word "kale."

Two other southern greens, also members of the genus *Brassica*, appear in Boston gardens. One is a white mustard (*B. napus*), the other is the turnip (*B. rapa*). Because the turnip, like the carrot, is a biennial, it can be left in the ground over the winter and in spring will send up a fresh top which can be cut as "spring greens."

Finally, a number of West Indians who have settled in Boston have set out asparagus beds (*Asparagus officinalis*) as well as the usual Afro-American vegetables. Several species of asparagus grow wild in the Mediterranean, and the Greeks may have used one or more of these plants as medicines. Our name for the plant is much like the Greeks' *asparagos*. The Romans definitely ate both cultivated and wild asparagus, and from Rome cultivation spread to Muslim Spain, Syria, and Egypt. These cultivated plants reentered Europe in the fifteenth century and reached the New World in the seventeenth.

The methods used in Boston's Afro-American community gardens reflect both their American and southern origins. Like New Englanders, the Afro-Americans garden on the flat, only staking up the pole beans and the tomatoes. Many do, however, hill up their rows, cultivating about the roots of the plants and making a deep furrow between the lines of the vegetables. In the heavy clay soils of the southern states, this technique encourages deep rooting and breaks up the baked top ground. It also makes a channel for irrigation. Nevertheless, Boston community garden plots cannot be conveniently arranged for irrigation; watering is by can, hose, and sprinkler.[19]

The Italian Garden

The Italians have brought long-standing and highly skilled traditions of intensive gardening to the United States. In common with the Chinese, though not to the same degree, Italians stake up plants and have vertical as well as horizontal gardens. Like the Chinese, too, Italian-Americans are extremely attentive, watering, weeding, cultivating, and trimming up their plants in daily visits.

Italy, as a Mediterranean country, sits in the midst of one of the five world centers of plant diversity, the others being Persia, India and the Malay Peninsula, the mountains of central China, and the spine of mountains from Mexico to Peru.[20] Consequently, many modern garden vegetables are either Italian variants, like broccoli, zucchini, red beets, and Savoy cabbage, or are ancient residents in Italian gardens, like peas, radishes, and lettuce.

Although Italy, and especially southern Italy, suffered, and continues to suffer, the terrible problems of a landless rural population, neither the national government nor the municipalities have devised an allotment program for those without private holdings. As in the United States, some industrialists in northern Italy furnished gardens with housing they erected for their workers. Also, in 1928 and 1929 the Fascists set up a leisure time program, *Opera Nazionale Dopolavora*, to give seeds, plants, and prizes to gardeners, but they did not go on to make land available to local associations of gardeners, as was then the practice in France, Germany, and other northern European countries.[21]

In recent years apartment dwellers in Italian cities have sometimes organized themselves to occupy vacant public land and to transform fringe city wastes into squatter gardens. In one case in Turin, on two successive nights in April 1975, six hundred "urban farmers" seized such a parcel, divided the land among themselves, laid out pathways and fences, set up garden sheds, and began cultivation. Yet municipal authorities in Italy still lack a uniform response to such popular demands for garden space. Turin agreed to negotiations and subsequently leased the gardens to the squatters. Other cities have experimented with formal allotments, but still others have forcibly cleared off the gardens and their gardeners.[22]

In Boston the Italians grow onions, peppers, beans, beets, lettuce, and zucchini in common with most gardeners. One of the special tests of the Italian-American vegetable garden, however, is the tomato (*Lycopersicon esculentum*), which is very carefully tended. The Italians were the first, and for several centuries the only, Europeans to take the American tomato into their national cuisine. Within thirty-five years of the Spanish capture of Mexico City (1519), an Italian herbalist, Pier Mattioli, published an account of the new vegetable's use. He wrote that the tomato was eaten fresh "with oil, salt, and pepper," just as we eat it today.

The early Italian names for the plant, *mala peruviana* (Peru apple), *pomi d'oro*, *mala aura* (golden apple), and *poma amoris* (love apple) followed the plant through Europe, but despite such encouraging names northern Europeans and their North American relatives refused the new delicacy. A 1581 statement by a French herbalist recorded the northern prejudice: "These apples were eaten by some Italians," he wrote, "like melons, but the strong stinking smell gives one sufficient notice how unhealthful and evil they are to eat."[23] Undeterred by such nonsense, the Italians cultivated the plant and improved it for their own purposes. Since southern peasants boiled it down to make a thick paste, and dried it in the sun, they favored thick skins and meaty, dry, smooth-fleshed fruits. The plum and other varieties they developed are now being used by tomato breeders to make the indestructible and tasteless American supermarket tomato.

Eggplants (*Solanum melongena*) are another must in an Italian garden. Their large purple fruits and shiny skins make them perhaps the most beautiful of all vegetables. A relative of the tomato, the potato, and the deadly nightshade, eggplant was long thought poisonous by Europeans, who only learned to cook and eat it from the example of the Muslims. One medieval Islamic cookbook offered eighteen different recipes.

The plant was first domesticated in India, where there are now several related species which still exist as wild plants or which flourish as weeds. They vary in shape and color, and only a few varieties are cultivated in Europe and the United States. The eggplant first traveled east to China, where a round-shaped variety was recorded in the sixth century A.D. The Chinese later developed a white variety of their own. The Muslims carried the vegetable west. A visitor to Samarkand, a city in south Russia on the medieval trade route for silk between China and Europe, noted six varieties of eggplant in the thirteenth century. By the end of the fifteenth Europeans had learned to cook and eat it, and subsequently it became a full-fledged member of Mediterranean cuisines.

The Spanish and Portuguese carried the eggplant to the New World, where it received some new names. In the West Indies it is sometimes called a garden egg. But the long migration of the plant from India found its historical echo when nineteenth-century Indian laborers were imported to the Caribbean and gave the eggplant the name "brown-jolly," a corruption of the Bengali word *brinjal*.[24]

In addition to the common lettuces Italian-Americans plant *scarola* (*Cichorium endiva*), the crinkly-leafed salad, otherwise called curly endive. Its origin is uncertain. Some think it came from China and South Asia, in which case, like the eggplant, it moved west along the trade routes from India. The Greeks and the Romans cultivated it, but it disappeared from the records, and perhaps from cultivation, until the twelfth century. A related plant (*C. intybus*), wild chicory, also called blue succory, a plant with a flower like a blue dandelion, grows wild in Europe. During the nineteenth century these wild plants were cultivated for their roots, which were dried and ground as a coffee substitute.

Sicilian beet is Swiss chard, a white-rooted beet (*Beta vulgaris cicla*) grown for its leaves and used in soups and as greens. Americans call it by its French name, chard, but it is also known as seakale beet, and perpetual spinach. The last name describes its good-natured willingness to send up fresh leaves all summer long.

Chard's origin is probably the Mediterranean region. The ancient Greeks knew the vegetable but regarded it, and cabbage, as indigestible unless highly seasoned; they therefore referred to both as food for the poor. In the Middle Ages, however, chard became extremely popular as the standard green to put into soups.

Garlic (*Allium sativum*), one of the many types of onions, is essential to both the Italian and the Chinese cuisines, and it is an ancient cultivar in both regions. In the Mediterranean it appears with the earliest historical evidence. The Egyptian priests thought it was food for slaves and poor people, but the Greeks enjoyed it. Indeed, the famous physician Hippocrates liked it better than onions. The oil in the garlic which gives it its pungency contains sulfur, and from that substance come the plant's mildly antiseptic properties and its common use in old-fashioned medicine.

The Latin name for the whole genus of onions is the Roman name for garlic, *allium*. The Romans gave garlic to their slaves to make them strong, and issued garlic to their soldiers to make them courageous. It may be, however, that the garlic they ate was not the common garlic of today's gardens but *A. ampeloprasum*, a larger and milder species.

Most urban gardeners do not grow white potatoes (*Solanum tuberosum*) because good ones can be purchased cheaply in the market, but where garden plots are large they are sometimes grown for the luxury of fresh new potatoes during the summer and fall. In the big community garden in East Boston, Italian-American residents do set out potatoes, and it is fitting that they do so, since the Italians were among the first Europeans to appreciate this American plant.

There are dozens of species and varieties of potato, and a full range of colors from red and violet to yellow and white, which grow in the spine of mountains that runs from Mexico to Chile. Part of this congregation of plants is so long-descended as to be pre-human. The process of domestication, therefore, must have been accidental as well as conscious. Some of the modern species seem to have come as weeds in gardens and trash heaps, others by hybridization. Whatever the paths to human cultivation, potatoes were staple foods in the Andes for two thousand years before the Conquest, and there are potato-design pots that date from 800 A.D.

The Spanish brought the white potato to Europe in the 1530s, and it was noted as present in Italy by the 1550s. The ways the plant became an English and American colonial vegetable are not known. It is possible that some captain who seized a Spanish ship brought the plants to England, and there is a story that Sir Walter Raleigh's gardener grew some for him on his estate in Cork, Ireland. It was Ireland, after all, that first made the potato its staple. It even developed a special product, the whiskey *poteen*, from distilling the fermented tubers. Later on it was the Irish who taught the English and the Americans to use the plant. There were neither potatoes nor tomatoes in Bradford's Plymouth or Winthrop's Boston.

The Italian and the English names for the vegetable combine two early Spanish words. The Spanish adopted the Peruvian name *papas* for the white potato, and took over the Caribbean word *batata* for the sweet potato. Some Europeans confused the two sounds, and from that misunderstanding came the Italian *patata*, the English "potato," and the Swedish *potatis*.

The Chinese Garden

The Chinese of Boston are most commonly immigrants or descendants of immigrants from south China, especially the region around Canton and Hong Kong. The area has a warm, wet climate and was blessed with a great variety of native plants. In addition to these Asian natives, the Chinese borrowed crops from every region of the earth, so that south China is a world vegetable catalogue. There is no tradition in China for allotment gardening, no provision of gardens in cities for those who do not own land, but there has been a very long tradition of urban agriculture, both in the form of gardening in small city parcels and in market gardening at the edge of town.[25]

The staples of the south of China are rice (*Oryza sativa*), soybean (*Glycine max*) curd, and various kinds of cabbages (*Brassicas*). Sweet and chili peppers from the Americas have become major crops, and carrots are also important, but the Chinese in Boston do not attempt such field crops in their community gardens. Instead, like everyone else, they raise delicacies, plants they remember as being at the heart of their favorite dishes and plants whose flavor is enhanced for being fresh out of the garden.[26]

At present old women predominate among Boston's Chinese community gardeners. Their preponderance results from the intertwining of old social rules and the anomalies of the U.S. immigration laws, which for decades prevented Asian families from settling in America. A social worker, Amy Wang, explained the situation. Years ago, in the province of Canton, the custom had been to send sons overseas in the hope that they might prosper and in time return to their communities and their families. So young men married and spent a year or so with their wives and then went abroad to work. The wives remained in China, separated from their husbands except for occasional visits, for twenty, thirty, and forty years. These couples reunited only when the U.S. immigration laws were reformed in 1952; but now, years later, many of Boston's Chinese wives are widows.

These women, trained by customs of a different place and era, do not visit around. They stick to home because they are concerned for their reputations. According to Chinese custom it was not proper for two women to talk alone in a room. The reason for this prohibition lay in the community's fear of gossip: what might the two women say about others? On the other hand, a respectable and well-mannered lady might come upon a friend accidentally, and in such a circumstance, the two friends might speak together as long as they wished. The community garden, then, serves a very important function as a place of unplanned meetings for Chinese women.

The typical Chinese garden is a selection from an enormous catalogue of south China vegetables. Greens, squashes, melons, beans, peas, and radishes predominate. Since Boston Chinese speak half a dozen different south China dialects, it is impossible to give a single spelling to a plant name. Many of the Chinese in Boston are from the Toishan region, a city about sixty-five miles south and west of Canton, so the plants will be signified in three ways whenever possible: in Toishanese, with an English common name if one exists, and in Latin.[27]

Chinese gardeners have a long list of greens to choose from: cabbages, mustards, spinach, chives, and parsley. Some of the best-known and most popular greens in Boston are the *bok toi* (*Brassica campestris chinensis*), a long cylindrical cabbage much used in stir-fry dishes. Cooked, the leaves are eaten like spinach; the white stems taste like asparagus. Another very popular green is the *guy toi* (*B. juncea*), a non-heading, white, branched mustard, called Chinese mustard. It can be used raw in salads or it can be cooked like spinach. The root is also edible and can be boiled and served like celeriac. It has a more peppery taste than the *bok toi*. There is also a Chinese broccoli, *guy lohn* (*B. alboglabra*), which is similar in flavor to the European types and like them is eaten stems and leaves. Many community garden plantings also include the cold-season Chinese celery cabbage, *dai toi* (*B. pekinensis*).

Chinese cooking depends on onions, and these are grown in many varieties. There are of course the common onions of biblical mention (*Allium cepa*) and garlic (*A. sativum*). Indeed, garlic is such an ancient plant in Chinese gardens that written Chinese gives it its own ideogram. These familiar onions are joined by a bunching onion with a hollow stem which grows in little clusters of four or five (*A. fistulosum*), the "Welsh onion." These scallions grew in eastern Asia, and in the Middle Ages they reached Europe, where the Germans called them *welsche*, meaning foreign onions. The British, being poor linguists, mistook the German for the sound of "Welsh," and henceforth they have been so labeled. A curiosity from the Chinese garden is the tree onion, or Egyptian onion (*A. cepa bulbiferum*), *tchung*, which sends out small bulbs on its flowering top. Finally, all south Chinese cook with *gow choi* (*A. odoratum*), a perennial garlic-flavored chive which has longer leaves than the common European chive (*A. schoenoprasum*), and the leaves are flattened toward their tips. The plant entered China at least two thousand years ago and was long regarded as an antidote to poison and a remedy for bleeding. Its oil does contain lots of sulfur, so it works as well, or as badly, as garlic.

Some of the Chinese garden plants are familiar to Americans because they are like plants known or used by everyone here. *Ho lan do*, snow peas (*Pisum sativum*, var. *macrocarpon*), are relatives of our common table varieties, and are becoming very popular in American gardens. *Ai gwa*, the Chinese eggplant (*Solanum melongena*), is just a narrow variety of our common egg-shaped vegetable. *Gum jum*, whose dried buds are stir-fried, is the "golden needles" day lily (*Hemerocallis fulva*). It was a cultivated Far Eastern plant which was imported to America, escaped the garden, and now grows wild across the United States.[28]

The *dow gauk*, the yard-long bean (*Vigna sesquipedalis*) seems more exotic. The bean grows wild in Africa and is cultivated in Europe and the United States as "cowpeas" for fodder and to improve the soil. Nevertheless, this bean is very nutritious and can be eaten fresh or dried. When grown on stakes, as with the community gardeners, the plants send out long, tender pods which can be cooked like our "French" string beans. The bean requires a hot summer, however, to perform well.[29]

Foo gwa is the bitter melon (*Momordica charantia*), a long, thin fuzzy vegetable which turns bright orange when it is fully ripe. Its pronounced bitterness comes from the presence of quinine in the fruit. When picked young, it stir-fries well, and it is often kept in brine to preserve it. The plant is also common in India, where it is used in pickles and curries.

Among the Chinese there is often an informal contest to see who can raise the largest *doan gwa*, or winter melon (*Benincasa hispida*). Otherwise known as the wax gourd or white gourd, the plant is a very ancient cultivar; indeed, its origins go so far back in time, it is doubtful if a wild ancestor survives. This light-skinned melon grows as large as watermelon. It can be steamed, or added to soups for its spicy taste. Also, if the shell is dried it can be made into a small kettle or bowl.[30]

Perhaps two dozen or more species of vegetables are commonly grown by the Chinese community gardeners in Boston. The methods the gardeners use are well adapted to working in tight urban spaces. The basic plan is dense and vertical. Vegetables are grown very close together in raised beds. The ground is first deeply dug to loosen up the bed, and then the soil is heaped up above the path level and supported at its edges by boards, sticks, and stones. The bed is never walked on. Because the seeds are sown so thickly, the plants require a great deal of water and fertilizer to flourish. Chinese-style gardening is thus an active sport with frequent waterings and fertilizings. Finally, everything of any size is tied up on sticks, brush, or fences so that it will take the least ground and catch the most sun. Such gardens often appear very disorderly to the casual passer-by, but the method is very effective.

The Hispanic Garden

It is fitting that a book that began with eighteenth-century land enclosures in England should end with a review of Hispanic urban gardening. The Caribbean, Mexican, and Latin American migrants who come to the cities of the United States today bring with them a similar experience of a powerless poor shifting about, seeking homes and jobs in the face of powerful forces which are transforming country and city. There is the same breakup of longstanding rural economies in the face of large-scale commercial agriculture; the same inability or unwillingness to mobilize national resources to make land available for city building; the same callousness about the exploitation of farm laborers and the collapse of small tenant farming; and the same prodigal waste of human skills and energies in the pursuit of the profits of urbanization and industrialization.

Whereas in England the relief authorities instituted the charitable allotment garden, in Latin America a variety of small-scale experiments are underway. In Panama the Ministries of Health and Agriculture are teaching mothers to garden in the yards around their houses. In Lima, Peru, the government and the local school of agriculture run demonstration gardens in the new city slums, community gardens are set up in conjunction with day care centers, and a foreign relief agency is teaching school children gardening. In Managua, Nicaragua, a German volunteer is using teenagers to tend allotment gardens.[31]

The two great social revolutions of Latin America, the Mexican revolution of 1910 and the Cuban revolution of 1959, loom over such small interventions. Both attacked the organization of land. In the Mexican case, the state confiscated the lands of the Roman Catholic Church and broke up a few foreign-owned large estates. Further, under the Ejido decree of 1915 and subsequent legislation, it made some grants of small parcels to landless peasants. These plots, like the English allotments, were designed to be only large enough to stave off starvation; they were not big enough to support an entire family in the absence of outside employment. The same program established a few community gardens in the towns of Mexico, but the reform was choked off by the political opposition and local terrorism of the large landowners.[32]

In the Cuban revolution of 1959 ultimately 79 percent of all the nation's farmland was brought under state ownership, and the remaining small private farms were organized into producers' cooperatives. During the process of nationalization the revolutionary government stumbled into all sorts of mistakes of management, but after twenty years it succeeded in putting a stop to the malnutrition of the Cuban population, an accomplishment unique in Latin America today.[33]

Yet for most Caribbean and Latin American migrants the urban experience is that of shifting for themselves. Waves of their countrymen have been moving toward the cities and forming rings of squatter settlements on the fringes and wastelands of San Juan, Mexico City, Caracas, and the like. Here encampments become shanty towns, and in time shanty towns are rebuilt by their residents to become regular urban quarters.[34]

Especially during the first years of squatter settlements, in the times when the municipal authorities are often hostile, it is only through cooperative work by the settlers themselves that they secure water, electricity, and other services. Although Hispanic immigrants to the United States have not repeated the land-seizure tactics of the squatter settlements, they do bring some of the same community spirit to their urban gardens. Here in Boston the gardeners at a South End community garden set aside a corner of their land for a community gathering place, and they built a shed for tools, cooking, and parties. It is a practice unique to their garden.

It is the climate of United States cities, however, that requires the most changes for Hispanic gardeners. Many are moving from subtropical regions to cold northern weather. Therefore, many of the plants that they would grow in a family garden down home must be forgone and substitutions made from the standard list of United States vegetables. Nevertheless, despite the climate, the emphasis on the ancient New World diet of corn, beans, and squash is preserved.

The largest group of Hispanic migrants to Boston is from Puerto Rico, so they bring to the city Caribbean preferences. Back home Puerto Ricans, both in the country and the towns, plant bananas, plantain, and pigeon peas to serve as screening and fences for their yards. They also set out coconuts, mangos, and lemon and orange trees as the umbrellas for a partially shaded tropical garden. Beneath this canopy they plant sweet potatoes, yams, taro, cassava, peanuts, amaranthus, okra, chili peppers, and tomatoes. Most of this preferred list of plants will not grow in a northern American city. Moreover, the very style of cultivation must be changed to meet United States conditions. In Puerto Rico, as in all tropical settings, gardeners practice intercropping, mixing together the fruit trees, the tall and short plants: the cassava and the squash, the peppers and the sweet potatoes, the corn and the beans. In the sun-poor north row cropping in full sun is the most successful technique.[35]

So, in Boston, Hispanic community gardeners plant lettuce, tomatoes, cabbage, onions, chives, eggplant, sweet potatoes, and corn like their fellow gardeners. Their ethnic specialties thus become the hot and sweet peppers, cilantro, a variety of beans, special squashes, and a yam.

It seems likely that the blandness of the New World diet of corn, beans, and squash made the native peppers an attractive addition to the Indian cuisine. However it came to pass, peppers (*Capsicum frutescens*) in the several varieties that grew in the Americas were cultivated and used before Columbus reached the Caribbean. The Spanish then carried the peppers home, and soon they spread through the Mediterranean and traveled to the Orient. Within fifty years of Columbus's first voyage four varieties were reported growing in India.

A thin, long pepper (*C. frutescens accuminatum*) is the essence of Latin cooking. Its common name, the chili pepper, comes from its Mexican Indian name. It is also known as the cayenne pepper, and it is the active ingredient in Hungarian paprika. In Spain the same pepper is known as the pimiento. More familiar to American gardeners than this hot pepper is the sweet, or bell, pepper (*C. frutescens grossum*) which is used unripe as a green pepper in salads and for cooking, and ripe as a sweet red pepper. There are also several other varieties of the plant, each with its own intensity of flavor. An acrid pepper, cone pepper (*C. frutescens connoides*), is grown in Louisiana for Tabasco sauce, and the red cluster pepper (*C. frutescens fasciculatum*) is so hot that it burns the hands of the pickers.

In the old Puerto Rican island diet the peppers entered each day's meals as an essential element in the *sofrito*. Country families made a sauce of peppers, chopped onions, green tomatoes, lard or pork fat, and spices. This sauce was added to the core dish of rice, beans, and codfish.[36]

In Boston one of the most important Hispanic community garden crops is cilantro (*Coriandrum sativum*), or in common American usage, coriander. The plant when young resembles parsley, and is used a great deal in Hispanic, Chinese, and Indian cooking. Indeed, there is such local demand that some gardeners market their cilantro. The leaves, if picked when the plant is small, can be added to soups and salads, or the plant can be left to grow to maturity (about two feet tall), and to send out its umbrella of small flowers and seeds. The ground seeds make a useful spice. Today they are an important ingredient in curries; years ago they were part of the recipe for flavoring gin.

Coriander is presumed to have had its origin in the Mediterranean, where it grows wild and as a weed, as well as being a cultivar. Its name in Latin, *coriandrum*, means bug. The association came from the odor the plant gives off when it is bruised. Drying the plant ends the off-smell.

Squashes (*Cucurbita* species) are among the most ancient of New World domestic plants. Remains of some have been dug up in sites which date back to 7000 B.C. As a group of plants they flourish wild as weeds, and as cultivars in Central America. The variety *C. pepo* comes in many forms ranging from the patty pan and yellow summer squash on to the pumpkin. Hispanic gardeners have brought two unfamiliar ones to the city, a round, yellow squash that they call by the general plant name *calabasa*, and a round, green one called *haullama*.

Only in the occasional large garden plots do Hispanic gardeners give over scarce space to corn, but all Hispanic gardeners plant several varieties of beans. The common American bean (*Phaseolus vulgaris*), like the squash, has many varieties. The *frijoles*, a white bean not unlike the Boston baked bean, the *frijoles negros*, black beans, the *habichuelas coloradas*, kidney beans, and the pinto beans with the spots are found in Hispanic community gardens. Also, as in Central America, gardeners plant the scarlet runner bean (*P. multiflorus*) as a vegetable, not just as an ornament.

Two rather different species of beans, less familiar to North Americans, are also common: jack beans (*Canavalia obtusifolia*) and *gandulas*, or pigeon-peas (*Cajanus cajan*). The origin of the jack bean is unknown, but it has been used in such scattered parts of the earth as the West Indies, Polynesia, and the Orient since the earliest historical times. Archaeologists in Mexico discovered such beans in places that date back to 3000 B.C. These beans have flat pods and edible leaves. In the West Indies they are known as "seaside beans," and seeds and pods are boiled together as you would an edible-podded pea.

The *gandulas* are natives of Africa or India. They were cultivated in Egypt before 2000 B.C. and in prehistoric India and Madagascar. The young seeds are eaten like a vegetable, cooked like a lima bean, and the mature seeds can be dried and split and used like a lentil. In Puerto Rico these beans are called *cajan*, or no-eyed peas.

Finally, like their Afro-American neighbors the Hispanic-Americans also plant sweet potatoes (*Ipomoea batatas*) and *ñame*, or yams (*Dioscorea trifida*). This last species is native to America and is often grown in the Caribbean. Unlike some yams, it does not bury its tubers deep beneath the ground but sends out about twelve sweet tubers near the surface. It is also known as the cushcush yam.

NOTES TO PART THREE

1. Norge W. Jerome, "Diet and Acculturation: The Case of Black-American In-Migrants," in Norge W. Jerome et al., *Nutritional Anthropology: Contemporary Approaches to Diet and Culture* (Pleasantville, N.Y., 1980), 275–325; Toronto Nutrition Committee, *Food Customs of New Canadians* (Toronto, 1967); V. M. Gladney, *Food Practices of Mexican Americans in Los Angeles County* (Los Angeles County Health Department, 1966); E. E. Rodert, *Food Practices of Arabic Background Families in East Valley District* (Los Angeles County Health Department, 1969).

2. Rachel Kaplan, "The Role of Nature in the Urban Context," in Irwin Altman and Joachim F. Wohlwill, eds., *Behavior and the Natural Environment* (New York, 1983), 150–51.

3. Margaret L. Arnott, *Gastronomy, Anthropology, and Food Habits* (The Hague, 1975), 91–111.

4. David A. Cleveland, Thomas V. Orum, and Nancy Ferguson, "Economic Value of Home Vegetable Gardens in an Urban Desert Environment," *HortScience* 20 (August 1985): 694–96.

5. Exodus 16:31; Numbers 11:7.

6. F. H. King, *Farmers of Forty Centuries, or Permanent Agriculture in China, Korea, and Japan* (Emmaus, Pa., 1911), 60–80; Peter Chan and Spencer Gill, *Better Vegetable Gardens the Chinese Way: Peter Chan's Raised Bed System* (Portland, Ore., 1977).

7. Edgar Anderson, *Plants, Man, and Life* (Berkeley, Calif., 1967), 112–17; *Sturtevant's Notes on Edible Plants*, U. P. Hedrick, ed., *Report of the New York Agricultural Experiment Station for the Year 1919* (Albany, N.Y., 1919).

8. Oakes Ames, *Economic Annuals and Human Culture* (Cambridge, Mass., 1939), 132–33; David Rindos, *The Origins of Agriculture: An Evolutionary Perspective* (Orlando, Fla., 1984), 138–89; and National Academy of Sciences, Advisory Committee on Technological Innovation, *Underexploited Tropical Plants with Promising Economic Value* (Washington, D.C., 1975).

9. Unless a special additional footnote is given, the histories of plants which follow were constructed out of the information given in the following books. Each book lists the vegetable under its Latin name, so all the data can be easily located without the necessity of page numbers. When additional sources were consulted, each source has been provided with its own footnote: S. G. Harrison, G. B. Masefield, and Michael Wallis, *The Oxford Book of Food Plants* (London, 1969); Yann Lovelock, *The Vegetable Book: An Unnatural History* (New York, 1972); Ames; and Edgar Anderson, *Plants, Man, and Life* (Berkeley, Calif., 1967). In those cases in which the authorities disagree, I have relied upon Anderson's interpretation. The late professor Anderson was for many years the director of the Missouri Botanic Gardens in St. Louis and an authority on the history of economic plants.

10. Claire Shaver Haughton, *Green Immigrants: The Plants That Transformed America* (New York, 1978), 200–204.

11. Nancy M. Page and Richard E. Weaver, Jr., *Wild Plants in the City* (New York, 1975), 17.

12. Some authorities have questioned the biblical references to cucumbers as a vegetable of ancient Egypt. They argue that the cucumber arrived in Europe from China around the first century B.C. *Sturtevant's Notes*, 208. The usual account is that of Haughton, 86–90; or Winifred Walker, *All the Plants of the Bible* (New York, 1957), 64–65.

13. Charles M. Rich, "The Tomato," *Scientific American* 239 (August 1978): 77–87.

14. Jane Strickland Hussey, "Plants of Plimouth Plantation" (1975, mimeo., in the Library of the Massachusetts Horticultural Society).

15. William G. Haag, "Aborigine Influence on the Southern Diet," *Public Health Reports* 70 (September 1955): 920–21.

16. Patricia J. O'Brien, "The Sweet Potato: Its Origin and Dispersal," *American Anthropologist* 74 (June 1972): 324–65; Stuart Berg Flexner, *I Hear America Talking* (New York, 1976), 33.

17. Ames, 44–49.

18. Andrew M. Watson, *Agricultural Innovation in the Early Islamic World: The Diffusion of Crops and Farming Techniques, 700–1100* (Cambridge, Eng., 1983), 58–61.

19. Vera K. Ninez, "Household Gardens: Theoretical Considerations on an Old Survival Strategy," in *Potatoes in Food Systems, Research Series, Report no. 1* (International Potato Center, Lima, Peru, March 1985); Tadeusz Lewicki and Marion Johnson, *West African Food in the Middle Ages According to Arabic Sources* (Cambridge, Eng., 1974).

20. Anderson, 78.

21. Lebert H. Weir, *Europe at Play* (New York, 1937), 271–72; Victoria de Grazia, *The Culture of Consent: Mass Organization of Leisure in Fascist Italy* (Cambridge, Eng., 1981).

22. Giovanni Brino, "Urban Farmers in Turin," *Space & Society* 5 (September 1982): 50–57; and Giovanni Brino et al., *Orti urbani a Torino* (Firenze, 1982). In 1986 Fabio Giavedoni and Aurelio Alaimo of the University of Bologna took photographs of the municipal, private, and illegal squatters' community gardens of that city. These pictures can be seen at the Rotch Visual Collections, Massachusetts Institute of Technology.

23. Rich, 77.

24. Watson, 70–71.

25. John Lossing Buck, *Land Utilization in China* (Nanking, China, 1937); Yoshinobu Shiba, "Ningpo and Its Hinterland," in William G. Skinner, ed., *The City in Late Imperial China* (Stanford, Calif., 1977), 391–439; Goran Aijmer, *Economic Man in Sha Tin: Vegetable Gardeners in the Hong Kong Valley* (Scandinavian Institute of Asian Studies, Monograph Series no. 43, London and Malmo, Sweden, 1980); Urban Resource Systems, "Urban Agriculture: Meeting Basic Food Needs for the Urban Poor, Shanghai, China," in *Urban Examples for Basic Service Development in Cities* (UNICEF UE-9, San Francisco, 1984), 29–32.

26. E. N. Anderson, Jr., and Marja L. Anderson, "Modern China: South," in K. C. Chang, ed., *Food in Chinese Culture* (New Haven, Conn., 1977), 321–26.

27. The most convenient guide to Chinese vegetables is Geri Harrington, *Grow Your Own Chinese Vegetables* (New York, 1978). The sources for the Latin and English equivalents to the Toisanese plant names are: Gretta Norton, "Zing choy ho Means Good Gardening," *BUG* (spring 1985), 14–15; Anderson and Anderson; *Oxford Book of Food Plants;* and G. A. C. Herklots, *Vegetables in South-East Asia* (London, 1972).

28. William Coon, *Dictionary of Useful Plants* (Emmaus, Pa., 1974), 174–75.

29. Ames, 62–64.

30. Ames, 86.

31. Urban Resource Systems, *Urban Examples for Basic Services Development in Cities,* 6–8; Vera K. Ninez, "Working at Half-Potential," *Food and Nutrition Bulletin* 7 (September 1985): 10–11; Julie Ogletree, "Urban Gardens Critical in Developing Countries," *BUG* (winter 1985–86), 24.

32. Frank Tannenbaum, *The Mexican Agrarian Revolution* (New York, 1929), 223–42, 249–59; Ramon Eduardo Ruiz, *The Great Rebellion: Mexico 1905–1924* (New York, 1980), 304–39.

33. Nancy Forster and Howard Handleman, "Food Production and Distribution in Cuba: The

Impact of the Revolution," in John C. Super and Thomas C. Wright, eds., *Food, Politics, and Society in Latin America* (Lincoln, Nebr., 1985), 174–98.

34. John F. C. Turner, *Housing by People* (New York, 1977).

35. Clarissa T. Kimber, "Spatial Patterning in the Dooryard Gardens of Puerto Rico," *Geographical Review* 63 (January 1973): 6–26; Vera K. Ninez, "Introduction: Household Gardens and Small-Scale Food Production," *Food and Nutrition Bulletin* 7 (September 1985): 2–4.

36. Lydia J. Roberts, "Nutrition in Puerto Rico," *Journal of the American Dietetic Association* 20 (May 1944): 299.

INDEX

Action for Boston Community Development, 24, 30
Advertising Club, 19
Afro-American community, 20, 23–24, 25, 26–27, 39
Afro-American garden, 102, 107–10
Alianza Hispana, 39
Allium ampeloprasum (garlic), 112
Allium cepa (onion), 106, 115
Allium cepa bulbiferum (tree or Egyptian onion), 115
Allium fistulosum (scallion), 106, 115
Allium odoratum (garlic-flavored chive), 115
Allium porrum (leeks), 106
Allium sativum (garlic), 106, 112, 115
Allium schoenoprasum (chive), 106, 115
Allotment gardens
  in Boston, 14–15
  in England, 10, 12, 41*n*17
  in Europe, 12, 13
  in Italy, 13, 110
  in United States, 14–15, 18–19
American Community Garden Association, 23
Ames, Oakes, 108, 109
Anderson, Mark, 29, 35
Anglo-Irish garden, 102, 103–7
Antinuclear movement, 20
Antiwar movement, 7, 20, 22
Arachis hypogaea (peanut), 108
Arndtsen, Beth, 34
Asian immigrants, 24

Asner, Eve, 22
Asparagus (*Asparagus officinalis*), 109–10

Baber, Morell, 29
Bailey, Augusta, 27, 29
Basil, 100
Beans, 101, 108, 110, 114, 117, 118; (*Phaseolus lunatus*), 108; (*Phaseolus vulgaris*), 102, 103, 105, 107, 108, 119; (*Vicia faba*), 105; (*Vigna sesquipedalis*), 115
Beautification, urban, 16, 33
Beets (*Beta vulgaris*), 103, 104, 107, 110
Belgium, allotment gardens in, 13
Bell pepper (*Capsicum frutescens grossum*), 118
Belladonna, 106
Benincasa hispida (winter melon), 116
Berkeley (Cal.), 22
Beta maritima (wild beet), 104
Beta petula (wild beet), 104
Beta vulgaris (beet), 104
Beta vulgaris cicla (Swiss chard), 112
Birmingham (England), 11
Bitter melon (*Momordica charantia*), 100, 115
Boston Common, 18, 19
Boston Globe, 19
Boston Greenspace Alliance, 34
Boston Natural Areas Fund, 33
Boston Redevelopment Authority, 3, 4, 6–7, 25, 28–29, 32
Boston School Committee, 26

1 2 3

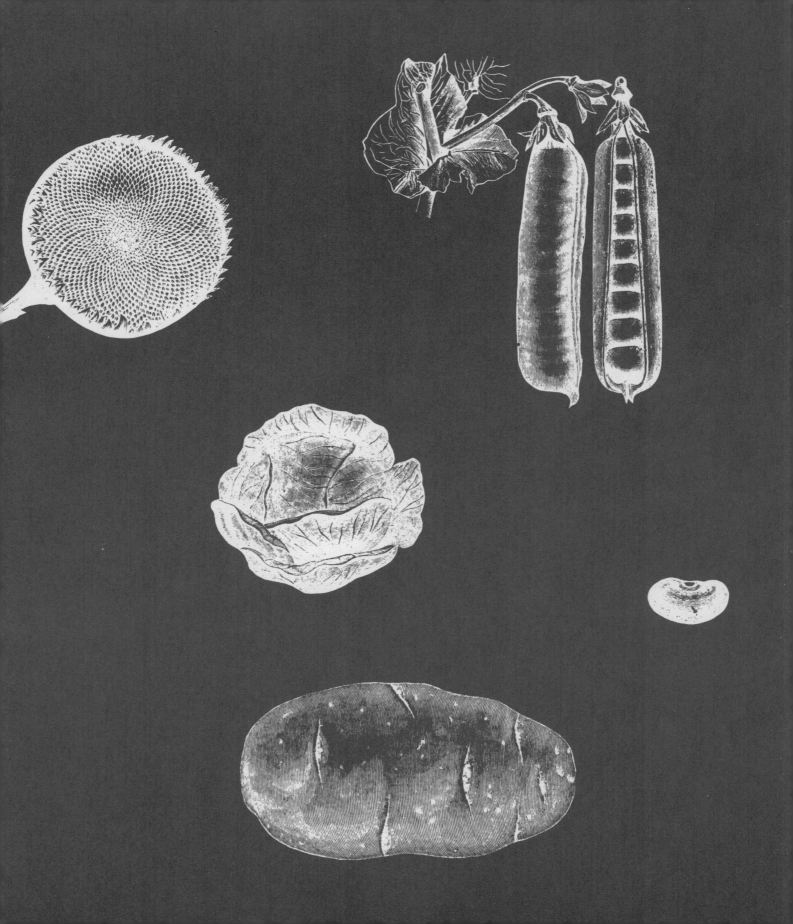